Lonely Traveller

Sereno Sky

Table of Contents

Special thanks to my dear wife, Eva, and to my son Marc for their proofreading and editing. Many thanks as well to all my dear friends on Tumblr, Facebook and in real life for all their encouragement!

"If we could help relieve someone or some animal from some suffering today, or making their life a touch easier with our kindness, then that day we lived was not in vain."

– Sereno Sky

Preface

A lot of thought, meditation and prayer have gone into this book. Things needed to be worded a bit carefully, as there are a lot of things about society and the way mankind is treating this planet and its inhabitants that I very much dislike. But I didn't want it to become a book that would manifest hate, because what this world needs most of all is the healing balm of spiritual love.

I have visited or lived in all the places the story leads you to. This novel describes authentic experiences of a young person in the 70s during the hippie days who is seeking a better world. The book offers a first-hand glimpse into the search many of the hippie youth went through. My hope is that the book will leave you, dear reader, with a touch more understanding and tolerance towards those around you who may question the way certain things are handled in this world.

Like A Rolling Stone

I was lying on my old mattress on the attic floor of our three-story building which included twelve apartments. When I say 'old mattress', it wasn't that I didn't have a real bed, but my real bed was down in my parent's apartment, and I had made myself a little hide-away up in the attic, and this old mattress was just fine for that.

It had been a long day at school. I was taking some time off to try to get my mind together and stay somewhat sane: Sane enough to go back down to our apartment to start the big pile of homework and preparing for tests. Sane enough to not forget the better times I'd had in my childhood when the world seemed so simple, so innocent. Sane enough to somewhat know why, and for what I was going to get up the next morning. Sane enough to put together my own ideology about life and what I believed should be the essence of it. Or maybe just sane enough to make it through that next hour.

I was listening to Bob Dylan. I had to keep the volume low as people in the building wouldn't have been very excited to hear loud music at eight in the evening. Nobody had complained about my hippie-hangout place I had created in my parent's attic. I shared a room with my brother downstairs. He was a couple years younger than me, and since the hippie-wave hadn't reached him yet, he was basically living in another world. It's not that we didn't get along, we basically always did, but I had gotten interested in totally different things in those days. Up there I could think my thoughts and feel my feelings and the place was filled with my thoughts and feelings only.

Well, not only that. It had my pictures from the Woodstock festival, of Janis Joplin, Carlos Santana, Jimmy Hendrix, and Joe Cocker hanging up on the walls. It had my music and my incense and my decorations. I had patterned cloths from the orient hanging all around. The whole place reflected my present self. I was wondering what the neighbours might have thought, if ever any of them had come up to get something from their attic. My parents knew I had made this hangout place up there, but it never became an issue and I don't remember them ever going up there to look at it. I appreciated the fact that neither they, nor anyone else in the house had made a scene about it.

"How does it feel...to be on your own...with no direction home...like a rolling stone." I was listening to one of my favourite pieces. I liked the tune; it reflected my mood. Most of all, the words were a pretty clear description of how I felt in those days. The fact that someone had translated such thoughts into words and music showed me that other people were having similar feelings about the world and life. Were my thoughts and feelings awakened by such music? Or was that kind of music just coming in as a comforting confirmation that I wasn't the only one feeling this way? It may likely have been a mixture of both.

How come there was a whole new generation of people that suddenly started thinking and feeling like that in those days? It was an interesting thought. Was it because of the cruel pictures flooding in from the Vietnam War? I had to stop watching the news program several times as I was repelled by the images. I didn't like any war, no matter what justifications or reasons were given.

Or was it because the world had sped up its industrialization with highways rolling over what used to be farmland and nature? Or because of all these factories shooting up like artificial mushrooms made of ugly concrete blocks? It seemed like a whole new generation had grown up seeing such big changes happening in a very short time span of about ten years. I was thinking that it's this constant push for more materialism which kills everything: It kills mother earth, its resources and its animals; it kills peace and love and is slowly killing people from the inside. Somewhere along the line of all these tremendous industrial and technological developments and changes, a new generation started feeling uneasy about it: The hippie movement was born!

'Like a rolling stone'. I was sitting on my old mattress and wondering how many people were feeling like that right now somewhere in their room, in the midst of a world they couldn't understand anymore. Woodstock attracted around 400'000 of them. But that's just counting the ones who could afford to somehow get up there. In Europe they had started similar festivals, like the Isle of Wight festival. I was just around thirteen years old when these festivals had happened, but I had seen an increasing amount of hippies in my city. You could see by the way they were dressed and let their hair grow. They just looked totally different from the norm.

But before going any further, let me introduce myself: My name is Bernardo. I was born as the oldest of four siblings in a Swiss bilingual city along the language border. Part of the people spoke French, the other German, and most signs were written in both French and German. Like the sign 'bakery', for example, would be written in both languages to make no one feel left out.

I led a somewhat regular childhood in a lower middle class environment, where my Dad had to work very hard to make a living, considering that with four kids Mom couldn't go to work but needed to stay home. In those days one could still sort of do that, if he worked all kinds of extra hours and had all kinds of side jobs, which my Dad did. And why does the name Bernardo have a somewhat Italian flavour? Perhaps my parents wanted to make one of my grandmas happy who was of Italian origin, or maybe it was just one of those names that were in fashion that year.

I remember my early childhood was one filled with lots of nice memories, such as gardening with my Dad on the vegetable plot he had rented close to our apartment, visiting grandparents regularly, and doing lots of fun activities with my childhood friends. We used to go hiking a lot with my parents and mushroom hunting in the season, as well as berry-picking. With four kids this brought in quite a bit of naturally grown food. In winter my parents took us skiing and I was very passionate about it, even doing competition.

I was doing well at school and was especially good at languages, geography, history and singing. Being really interested in those things made my initial years at school quite easy. There isn't actually anything spectacular or earth-shaking to mention until my skiing accident. That accident had me stuck for six long weeks at the hospital and unable to move, and then the same amount of weeks at home in bed with a cast on my leg. When I was finally able to go back to school, I had missed out on a lot. Having been a good student before and now having so much to catch up with was a big discouragement for me.

Eventually I was able to catch up to my former momentum, but a lot of fun had gone out of my life. All those of you who may have had a similar accident or mishap can probably relate to what a deep impact such misfortune can have on one's life.

During the same time big choices needed to be made regarding my future professional direction. Various options were laid out before me: teacher, business, languages, journalism. I visited all kinds of companies in those days as part of a program to help us young people decide what to do with our career lives. I ended up attending a high school for commerce and trade as my good grades gained me access without needing to take the customary exam. I hated exams and was glad I was able to escape one. I was informed that I could still switch to becoming a teacher later if I wanted to. Everyone, my parents and teachers, had given me advice on my future. The direction I chose seemed to be the lesser evil for the lonely traveler I was, as I honestly had no clue as to what I wanted to become or do in this world.

So, how did I first learn about the hippies? Well, when I had been in hospital I had so much time to listen to music and one of the other fellows in the room was really into the Rolling Stones, the Beatles and stuff. I remember the first hippies in my home-town, they looked cool, but there seemed to be a bit more to it than that, because in order to dress and look the way they did, one had to sort of not care about what other people thought about it. While we still lived at home, on the bread and butter of our parents, we couldn't really do what we wanted. Growing my hair long and putting on hippie clothing could have become major points of disputes with them. These were delicate times in regards to getting along with parents; I guess they still somewhat are. So in that sense I admired young people who dressed the way they wanted or guys growing their hair long. Fortunately for them, they were a bit older than me and could probably afford to go against the will of their parents.

Slowly, or quickly if you wish, my views started clashing with the general views of society due to the influence of the hippie-movement, the Vietnam War, Woodstock, spirituality, Jesus, Buddha, Hinduism, drugs, sex and rock n' roll. I felt I was 'born to be wild' and if I was going to turn my back on society I might as well go all the way. Whether other people thought it was cool mattered less and less as long as I myself felt it was cool.

'Sex, drugs and rock n' roll' was one of the credo of the hippies, at least for some. I guess I belonged more to the category of 'feelings, psychedelics, spirituality, and nature.' But it didn't matter that much in those days because we all just wanted something different from the materialistic treadmill we had been born into, and we all got along.

I guess a general view among many young hippies was that society had become so materialistic, and so destructive of mother earth, that it was necessary to get out of that system in order to find new, more peaceful and spiritual ways and alternative lifestyles. The kinds which would allow a person to live freer, and in accordance with their ideas and beliefs, not just following the general materialistic dog-eat-dog trends of society.

"Bernardo, I'm going to hitchhike to Amsterdam!" George was one of my first hippie friends that I had while still studying and living with my parents. I must add that in those days I started having a whole new set of friends other than my colleagues at school, or my old football buddies from my neighbourhood, as they didn't suit my present ideology anymore. Anyone with long hair was considered a potential new friend. We would hang around a certain coffee shop called 'Liberty', where we would meet after school or work. That's where I got to know lots of new friends and we would listen to our kind of music there. Someone must have realized that with more and more hippies around, opening such a coffee place could fulfill a demand, and it did. There was a small side street close by where we'd go and smoke our first joints, away from curious eyes, then go back to the coffee shop. So by going there regularly I soon had a totally new set of friends, including George.

LONELY TRAVELLER

I had been working at some side-job for students, and it was time for summer holidays. My parents were told that I would go on a trip with George, whom they didn't even know, and we'd be going by train. Of course that was dishonest, but how could one tell his parents he was going to hitchhike to Amsterdam and meet hippies. Hippies were considered a big disaster by society, and I didn't want to worry my parents unnecessarily.

Hitchhiking worked great in those days. Some hippies had cars, and they would often paint them, so if you saw one of those cars approaching, you could be quite sure they'd stop and ask where you needed to go. There were also a lot of people who just wanted to be helpful, and it was still quite safe to take people along, as crime wasn't a big problem in Europe at that time.

After a night in our sleeping bags somewhere along a German highway, we arrived in Amsterdam the next day. The city was well-known among hippies as some sort of hippie mecca, not only to us Europeans, but also to hippies from all over the world, mostly because of its somewhat liberal views on marihuana and towards hippies in general.

Entering the city was amazing, even just because of the fact that I had never been up north. With my parents we had always travelled south when we left the country, to the southern beaches in Italy and France. Amsterdam is a very interesting city with lots of canals flowing through it, a bit like the Venice of the North.

The first thing I noticed was the many backpackers like us. We used to travel with a backpack and

sleeping bag, which was all we needed. Taking anything else along would have only made it heavier to
carry and more difficult to catch a ride. We were
headed the same direction the other backpackers were:
To 'Dam Square'. This is something like the main plaza
in Amsterdam and had been totally taken over by the
hippies. It consists of some kind of monument with all
these round circles, forming platforms like stairs.
When we got there we put down our backpacks and
felt like we had arrived at the center of the hippie universe.

Why the city would let the hippies besiege their
main monument and plaza was something I was wondering about, but for the moment I just wanted to take
in this wonderful feeling and all the good vibes which
this situation offered. Some folks were playing the guitar while others were playing bongos or playing a
flute. Travellers with long hair were arriving constantly from all corners of the world, and I just wanted
to go around asking everyone where they had been to,
and listen to all their exciting stories of interesting
places they had visited around the world. I still remember my first arrival at 'Dam Square' as being one
of the most exciting days of my whole youth.

There was a massive exchange of information taking place as people would share their experiences from
various hippie meccas they had been to, about affordable places to stay at and cheap ways to travel. I remember various books had been written on 'how to
travel Europe on five dollars a day', and I'd seen quite
a few people referring to one of these books for their
travels.

LONELY TRAVELLER

'Like a rolling stone', but suddenly I felt for the first time like I wasn't rolling alone, and that there was a worldwide wave of young people rolling along with me.

Hippie Mecca

Vondelpark was the other main hippie-hangout place in Amsterdam and towards the evening all backpackers and hippies started moving that direction, so we just went along. When we got there, I was so amazed to find thousands of hippies having put their backpacks and sleeping bags down around the small lakes of the park. I'd never seen anything like this and I could literally feel hippie vibes flowing all over me and the air definitely smelled like love and peace. I could hear guitars, music, bongos and flutes everywhere and people saying: "Hey man! Where are you from"?

Imagine a European city opening its main city park to the 'dirty' hippies coming from all around the world and allowing them to sleep there, play music there, smoke marihuana there, have sex there. It gave me a lot of sympathy for the Dutch people, a sentiment I still feel to this very day.

And not only this: For times when it would rain, which happens often in central and northern Europe, the hippies didn't need to sleep in Vondelpark where it would get muddy. The city of Amsterdam had turned a few old factories and facilities into hippie youth-hostels which were called 'sleep-ins'. A 'sleep-in' usually consisted of hundreds of metallic beds, a 24 hour reception and a bar that was open all night, offering cheap snacks and drinks and a place to hang out on old sofas. There were showers, toilets and a luggage counter where you could deposit your luggage if you wanted to go around town. I don't remember the exact price per night, not even today's search engines seem to remember, but it was very cheap. And the 'sleep-ins' were run by hippies, so one really felt at home there.

Next to 'Dam Square' was a street where many hippies were holding up signs, advertising their needs or something to sell. You could see signs like: 'Need a trip to Nepal'....'Camper to sell'... 'Need companion to go to Spain'...'Who will travel with me to Morocco'. Everyone was going somewhere, but no one wanted to settle; people were on the move in those days, and so was I.

Now it's being said that hippies were illusionists, escapists, not really offering any solutions themselves. All that didn't really matter to us. We were just fed up, and thought that if we just got away and created our own world, then at least we didn't need to be a part of a society that we didn't believe in.

The next day we went to the famous Amsterdam flea-market and I got a couple really nice hippie clothes. That flea-market was a real hippie-bazaar in those days, and hippies brought stuff they had acquired on their trips to India, Nepal, Afghanistan and Morocco. Fashion had not yet gotten involved with the hippie-trip, which was nice, and hippie-fashion was a world of its own. If you had a pair of jeans, you would wear them all the time, and of course wash it sometimes so that it would get that washed-out look, and the more ragged and used it started looking, the better it was. We were totally not into the latest fashion.

I had actually gone to see my grandma a while back and had asked her if there were still some clothes from grandpa who had died a few years before, and she was very happy to have me go look in the attic to see if I'd find something. There was this old wooden trunk way up under the roof, with some light shining upon it through a small window. To me it was like a treasure box. There were old hand-woven natural sweaters and cool jackets, stuff that had lasted for years and was going to last a few more on me. We didn't feel weird at all to put on old clothing from our ancestors, on the contrary. I was sort of proud to wear stuff that was still in good condition instead of letting it rot away and buy new stuff. Why should old stuff be so discarded by society? It's encouraged by commercialism to always need new things.

Then I had this Nepali or Indian bag which I had purchased in a hippie shop. In there was my flute, my blues-harp harmonica, cigarettes, a book as I would often read something, and a shilom (a shilom was a clay pipe for smoking marihuana). In winter we hippies would wear some old warm coats from a few generations back which we often would find on a flea-market, as well as sheep coats from Afghanistan, which were quite popular among us, and I wore one of those. Needless to say we looked quite wild, but we didn't mind that at all. There was admittedly also a certain element of provocation in our appearance as we didn't want to follow the commercial trends that fashion tried to impose on young people.

That evening, back in Vondelpark, George and I met two lovely hippie-girls from Finland who were travelling Europe by train. That was a very popular thing to do back then, especially for girls who didn't want to take the risks involved in hitchhiking. One could purchase this ticket for all of Europe for one month or so and travel all around Europe with it.

I got on really well with Lina, she was a year younger than me and we were talking endlessly. It seemed we had a lot in common, the way we looked at things and the world. She was studying to become a nurse and had taken the summer holiday to travel Europe with her girlfriend. We must have spent half the night talking, and I could tell she liked me. When we finally lay down for some sleep, she cuddled up and slept very close to me. It was the first time I had slept next to a girl outdoors. They left the next morning as they had a planned route, but we did exchange addresses. It would take a while until we'd hear from each other again.

The next morning, after the girls had left, it started raining, so we thought it was time to go find one of the famous 'sleep-ins' where we would be safe from the rain and wetness. The park was getting empty and it seemed like all the hippies were heading towards the 'sleep-ins' in order to deposit their belongings to keep them from getting wet, and to book a bed for the coming night.

After entering and paying the small fee, you could find yourself a bed, which meant sometimes on a double bunk-bed, and since I have a bit of difficulty with heights, I would usually try to get one on the bottom. I liked that the bedrooms were mixed, and only the toilets and showers were separate. There was music playing at the bar and the large hall was filled with a bunch of old sofas, which looked like they had been donated by some people for this 'good cause'.

We stayed in Amsterdam for about a week. Returning home from this trip was a bit of a downer. It became even more obvious that my new lifestyle had 'run out of style' in this society and I was eagerly embracing my new hippie-world and the worldwide hippie movement. My parents weren't too happy with the ongoing changes they had obviously noticed. So I tried to keep my new life-style as low-key as possible when I was at our house, as it wasn't my intention to hurt them.

In retrospect, I guess the parents of the hippie-generation had it quite difficult. Before that time people were sort of used to do what their parents wanted, and the term 'alternative lifestyle' had probably not even existed before. I think most parents were a bit ill-prepared for such monumental changes of a whole youth movement turning against traditions and society. In that sense I felt really sorry for my parents, and I am thankful that even though this must have been very difficult for them, they always treated me very fairly.

Parents usually only want the best and happiness for their kids. But the hippies were the first generation turning against their parents. Why? Because we didn't feel happier in having gadgets, in having materialism, in having financial security. Our happiness was based much more on friendship, love and peace in this world. And it was based on seeing dear mother earth and its nature and animals not being wasted away. So that's the sort of happiness we wanted! One can't really blame parents for that though, as it's the whole system that would need to be turned around.

Life went on with school and studying. I would still meet my friends after school and was less and less interested in studying, which wasn't that great; but it was as it was. At that time, Carol became my girlfriend. She was a year younger than I and was part of the circle of close friends I had made during that time. I remember when she told me that her mother wanted to meet me. I was a bit scared, as being a hippie was not such a great asset in those days with parents of girlfriends, but her mother took it well. She wanted to make sure her daughter started taking the pill as apparently she hadn't had sex before she met me. I hadn't had any serious relationship until then either. Somehow none of them had lasted longer than a month or so. This was probably my fault, as I was looking for a real hippie-girl, and Carol was the first one who got pretty close to that.

I was also getting quite involved with a band, and was their singer for a while. We never got as far as giving a concert, as none of us really had much time to dedicate to rehearsals because we were all studying. But the band-members became good friends of mine and we usually spent the weekends together, as well as spending once a week practicing, which of course wasn't enough to get anywhere musically.

I went back to Amsterdam a few times during the coming years. I always felt very happy and excited to be there. For me going to Amsterdam was not just hanging around smoking dope, though I did that too, but it was an opportunity to get to know other hippies and their views on the world. I was just so hungry in those years for some input about travelling, about views for a better world and about spiritual experiences people had made, things that had brought them closer to inner peace in their search.

Another place I went to a couple of times in Holland is Haarlem at the North Sea coast where there are beautiful sand dunes. Many hippies gathered there as well, as you could sleep out in the sand dunes with your sleeping bag. Unfortunately, I had a really bad 'trip' there caused by some so-called hippies who had told me all kinds of lies they had agreed on, in order to get me all confused. They seemed to have a fun time about it. I would never understand people who could have fun at the expense of others by hurting them physically or spiritually. From that moment on I started being much more careful about who I would take drugs with. This bad experience made me lose my innocence and trust in people. I started being quite a bit more skeptical towards others and checking out their motives a lot more. I came to the realization, that not every young person who looks like a hippie has necessarily pure, loving and kind motives, sad to say.

On one of my trips to Amsterdam I ran short of money as I wanted to go up to Denmark where there was also a large hippie-community at that time. So I took my flute and went to one of the main shopping streets in Amsterdam, sat down on the side of the street and started playing. To my amazement people actually really liked it and the coins were just dropping on my bag like crazy. It went great for some time, and I was really concentrating on my flute and the melodies I was playing. Suddenly I saw four legs in uniform standing in front of me. They were kind, but still needed to take me to the police station and confiscated my flute, to make sure I was not going to play on the main walking street again, which is sort of understandable. I guess they couldn't afford to have all the hippies playing music on the main walking street; that might have been a bit too much to expect. I was very sad though about the loss of my beautiful flute.

They also found some 'shit' (hashish) on me which I had bought at 'Dam Square'. It was actually the first time I had bought that stuff, as before I'd usually just bought marihuana. So I wasn't so familiar with 'shit', and sure enough, the police smelled it and said: "Someone sold you some real cow-shit". They laughed and were actually very kind to me, which reflected the general openness the Dutch people seemed to have in those days towards us hippies.

During those school years, I also hitchhiked with Carol to Amsterdam. It was actually nice to hitchhike with a girl, as I could sit down with our backpack and just let her stand in front and cars used to stop immediately. Of course by the time the car door was open I showed up too, ha! I enjoyed showing Carol all the places in Amsterdam. We slept one night in Vondelpark and a couple of nights in a 'sleep-in'. Some 'coffee-shops' had been opened a while back and we went to visit them. They were quite big, like the 'Melkweg' and the 'Paradiso', with lots of hippies having small stands and selling their different 'herbs'. They definitely looked much more like a hippie-bazaar than a coffee-shop, it was great! And on top of it the city permitted it, so no one was in fear of police-raids. These coffee-shops were great places for meeting a lot of hippies and finding some nice grass for a good joint, as well as listening to good music.

Born To Be Wild

Towards the end of my commercial high-school I was getting really itchy feet to start some major travelling. As soon as school was finished I moved out of my parents' place. I started getting temporary jobs in order to make some money and together with some of my best friends, we were miraculously able to rent an old house down-town which was going to be torn down in a couple of years. It had three floors and on each floor there was an apartment with a kitchen, bathroom and about three bedrooms. It had a great roof-terrace where we used to go skinny dipping and none of the neighbours could see it as it had walls around.

So in order to get the rent together every month, we needed to find others to move in, and eventually we were about a dozen people living in that house and often more. There was a constant in and out of hippies every day. and guitar music mixed with various sounds coming from the different rooms, such as Pink Floyd, Genesis, Santana, Cat Steven, Jethro Tull, Deep Purple, Led Zeppelin.... We still occasionally listened to the ones who had helped initiate the hippie music, such as Bob Dylan, the Doors, Beatles, Rolling Stones,

Grateful Dead, Janis Joplin, Jimmy Hendrix and others. But we had all still been quite young and 'good' school boys and girls when these musicians and bands had their day, and we knew Woodstock only from the movie. Many new bands had appeared since then and of course if some new album would come on the market we would listen to them day and night. It was during that time that I went to a Pink Floyd concert, and it's still my favourite band today.

At some point some of my friends and I got into an Indian guru trip. Many hippies did in those days including the Beatles. This one group had established an 'Ashram' (monastery for meditation) in our city, and one could go there to meditate or follow meditation-classes. I was reading various pieces of literature related to Hinduism, yoga and meditation in those days, as well as practicing them. Later on I followed some of the 'Mahatmas' around, along with a group of other hippies.

A couple years earlier I had visited a variety of Christian groups to check them out too. As you can see, I was checking out different religions. I felt that one needs to do a bit of studying around the source in order to find out what truth there was originally in there, and to extract the spiritual value if there was any.

After my high-school was finished, I felt such an urge to get away, as mentioned before This time I didn't want to go to Amsterdam; I wanted to go visit other hippie-hangouts. I felt the need for sunshine and the beach, but also to just get away from it all to a quieter place, like Formentera. One of my friends from the band at home had told me about it. He had been there a couple months before, and I had already heard about that island on my previous travels to Amsterdam. Formentera lies right next to Ibiza, and both islands belong to Spain and are located out in the Mediterranean Sea. My plan was to go for three to four weeks, since I didn't have enough money for staying longer anyway. But it should help me to re-evaluate what I should do with life, now that I had finished my basic studies. And a quiet hippie-island seemed just right for doing that.

Carol didn't want to come with me, not even for a couple of weeks. Prior to this, I had started feeling that our relationship had sort of had its run; our interests started being too different. I had itchy feet to travel, and she could feel that, which probably made her feel insecure. She didn't feel like wanting to travel and was more concerned about her professional career. We had no big official end-of-relationship talk. We didn't need to.

Shortly before leaving I received a letter from Lina, the Finnish girl whom I had met in Amsterdam. She had written me that she was going to be in Southern France this summer as another family had invited her to go with them. Since Carol was cooling off with me and didn't want to come on this trip anyway, I had written Lina that I could pass by and see her on my way down to Spain. The day before leaving, another letter from her was in the mail with the phone-number of the place she was going to be staying at in Southern France, near Sète.

'Bernardo...concentrate on your hitchhiking', I thought to myself as another car passed by and didn't stop to take me. 'You're thinking too much about life'.

Indeed I was. I had finished high-school but had no idea what I was supposed to do in the future, and I was wondering if this trip was somehow going to give me more clues. The situation with Carol also hurt quite a bit somewhere inside. Anyways, maybe this time away was going to clear up some of these clouds.

'That hippie bus didn't take me, it was full'. Usually one could count on the hippie cars to be happy to stop and give a ride. I had taken my backpack and a sleeping bag, the same as I used to take with me to Amsterdam, but this time the trip was south, hitchhiking down from the border near Geneva. Suddenly, someone put on the breaks, stopped, and even drove back a few meters to ask me where I needed to go. I felt quite relieved; I was finally on my way.

I was picked up by a French businessman from Lyon, who had done some business in Switzerland that morning and was on his way home. "Two hours to Lyon", he said. That is really how hitchhiking was in those days: He had someone to talk to and I had a free trip to Lyon. Today, people are much more scared to do hitchhiking, the world has gotten more evil and with more crime. Nowadays many people use cameras around their houses. Crazy world!

When I got out in Lyon I felt that warm south wind blowing in my face streaming up from the 'Rhone Valley', and the exhilarating feeling of freedom. Some other kind hearted people took me further south, and by late evening I had reached Avignon. I ended up sleeping under the famous 'Pont d'Avignon', a medieval bridge that only has a few arches left as the 'Rhone River' had washed most of the bridge away during the floods.

LONELY TRAVELLER

After leaving Avignon I headed towards the 'Camargue', an area in Southern France which is famous for its wild horses. I had a couple of days left before Lina would be arriving in Sète, and I had always wanted to see the wild horses there. But there were so many tourists in the middle of summer with endless rows of cars parked. Nevertheless, after asking around for directions, I did finally get to see a herd of wild horses galloping along the beach. They were so beautiful and seemed to be so free. It made me think of the song 'Wild horses' from the Rolling Stones. Perhaps being a wild horse wouldn't be such a bad choice for my next life, if there was reincarnation. I had found a vantage point up on a small sand dune and there were quite a lot of people watching. I ended up sleeping right there that night all by myself. I was happy to leave the next day as there were just too many tourists around for my liking.

So after getting up and grabbing myself a coffee somewhere on the way back to the main road, I headed towards Sète where I was going to meet up with Lina. It was afternoon when I arrived there. I found my way to the beach where I was planning on spending the next night. After sunset, there was a fire and some music, surrounded by some hippies and 'clochards'. These are some form of French vagabonds who live nowhere and everywhere. Mainly older men wearing shaggy clothing, accompanied by their dogs and a bottle of wine, who definitely don't seem to want to go to a home for the elderly. They were sharing their food with us hippies and telling us stories about a UFO that had landed where they were sleeping, with some kind of creatures coming out and being very friendly with them. They had endless stories to tell from a lifetime on the road. Anyways, I could sleep safely there among these sweet people. It felt so peaceful falling asleep beside the sea, with the waves quietly splashing to the shore that night.

In the morning I went to call the number Lina had sent me and found out that they were expected to arrive soon. When I finally got to speak to her she was so happy and told me she would come down to the beach camp. About an hour later I saw her coming down the small road, with the soft wind of the sea blowing gently through her blond curly hair. We exchanged warm hugs and kisses; it felt so good to meet again. We talked for hours that night and listened to the fire nearby, to the waves splashing ashore and cuddling up closely. I felt closeness to her that I had not felt with Carol, and I was so glad she was able to stay with me that night.

The next day she had to go back to the house she was staying at to get some of her stuff. The family she was staying with apparently didn't mind her going to stay with her 'boyfriend', and when she came back we proceeded to find a quieter place away from the crowd. There were some cliffs nearby, with caves and natural platforms overlooking the sea. It was so amazing we decided to stay there. A backpack, a sleeping bag, a few t-shirts and towels make things at least halfway soft on a rocky cliff. But the breathtaking view of the endless sea with the waves crashing against the rocks sure made up for any discomfort. So did the sweet company, the soft touches, kisses, and endless embraces that we shared in the days we had there together.

Lina went back to the house each day to make sure that the family she had come with wouldn't worry about her, and she'd bring some food back each time. We'd spend some time at the beach with the other hippies, swimming in the sea and sitting around the fire talking at night, while listening to the guitar music someone was playing. We lay down on the soft sand at night and gaze into the stars, talk about life and what each of us were looking for, until the soft splashing of the waves would put us to sleep.

I told her about my search, which I felt had intensified since I started this trip. At one point she said: "We're all looking for something, it's a very individual road. I know what I want to do. I want to become a nurse and help people in that way." I always admired nurses. They don't have a big academic title, but they care for people every day. "I'm glad that your road is so clearly laid out before you, I wish mine were as well." She looked at me with a smile: "Bernardo, I don't think you look so completely lost. There is a lot inside of you and one day it's all going to come out". I thought about that a lot during years to come. "Maybe," I said, "I guess society puts a certain pressure on us to decide very early in life what we should do, but for some of us it just seems to take a little longer."

A few days later the family who Lina had been staying with wanted to go for some excursions in Southern France, visiting different sites, and they wanted her to go along as she was under their care. Somehow she must have felt that my journey must go on. We decided to stay in touch by mail, but we never saw each other again after that. A couple months later

I would receive a letter from her. She was back at her studies and had found a steady boyfriend.

I arrived in Barcelona around lunchtime the following day and found my way down to the port where I booked myself a ticket on the overnight ferry to Ibiza. With time to spend, there were other travellers who were going to take that ride and we went together to the park overlooking the harbor. It was a pleasant view and one could see different ships leaving and arriving. We smoked a joint, but had to hide it when a couple of 'Guardia Civil' (Spanish national police) came around the corner. They were wondering if we were up to no good, but we said something like "we're tourists, just waiting for the boat". One did have a certain respect of the 'Guardia Civil' in those days; they looked like people you didn't want to mess around with. They will always be remembered for their very particularly shaped black caps.

Later on, the ship left and I enjoyed feeling the Mediterranean wind blowing through my hair. It was nice to have found a few buddies who were heading the same direction, and I seemed to get along really well with one guy in particular named Paul. He was about the same age as I was and came from England.

There weren't any real beds in the class I had booked, just canvas chairs, the ones you can usually find at tourist beaches. Some were out on deck and others inside, as it could get quite windy and chilly at night. The ferry from Barcelona to Ibiza took about nine hours. When we got to Ibiza our little group of hippies made its way up to the castle to enjoy the view. The only thing we didn't like was that about every few minutes a plane was landing. Mass tourism had reached Ibiza by that time. We were glad to leave that evening with the small boat that brought us to Formentera. I would have liked to see more of Ibiza too, but for now I just felt like I needed to go to a real quiet place. I was looking forward to some time away from the masses.

The trip on that small old boat from Ibiza to Formentera was fantastic. We passed by impressive rock formations along the coast of Ibiza and then cruised along into the sunset. The boat ride didn't take long, a bit more than an hour and we arrived in La Savina, the harbor of Formentera. By the time the boat got there I was eager to see the kind of 'population' this island had. Sure enough, in that sense it was very different from Ibiza. At the harbor there were hippies looking for directions, but it was a very relaxed and quiet atmosphere. Upon arrival, we got something to eat and then went to a nearby beach for the night.

If You Really Search For It You Will Find It

The first morning I woke up in Formentera to the sound of beautiful waves. The sun was already quite high and shining on my face. We went back to the port, had some coffee and then hopped on a bus to San Fernando. It had a restaurant and pension called 'Fonda Pepe', which was the main hippie-hangout place on the island. Hippies weren't flooding in like in Amsterdam, it was a lot quieter. It is being said that Bob Dylan, Pink Floyd, Chris Rea and King Crimson all had visited the island, maybe looking for some solitude for their creative work.

'Fonda Pepe' was the only place on the Island which was buzzing with hippies from all over the world. At the pool out in the back we noticed a lot of hippies from the States. "Hi there, nice to see more freaks coming", one of them greeted us from the pool. We treated ourselves to some drinks and sat down for a while. The sun was getting very hot by that time, and it was time to head for the beach. The whole island is surrounded by long-stretched white beaches, except for the south of the island, which has a mountain with cliffs dipping into the sea.

This time we headed for the other side of the island and the beach was not far at all. By this time there were only four of us, the rest having stayed at the pension. Paul was one of the guys who still remained and with whom I had already been talking quite a bit about our view of things. "This island is perfect to get away and think", he said. "I need to find out what I want to do when I get back to England. My parents want me to study and take over the business, but I would like to do something more creative." He had started painting as a hobby. "Then why don't you start here?" I suggested. "I will. I brought my pencil and paper with me."

He unpacked this A4 size wooden board, where he could just clip on a white sheet of paper and start. "I've already seen a lot of stuff I would like to do. I haven't got paint with me, but I'm going to do the coloring at home." He showed me some stuff he'd already done on his way down here. "This is beautiful, you definitely have talent." I actually enjoyed painting as well, but I had to admit it wasn't really my forte.

I had once asked the staff at one of the 'sleep-ins' in Amsterdam if they had some paint, as the entrance wall looked a bit grey and empty. They were happy that I wanted to paint something there and I gave them a faint idea of what I had in mind. So they had brought me a few cans of various colors of wall paint and I painted for a couple of hours. People actually really liked it.

The next day one of the Dutch guys took Paul and me for a bike ride on some of the bikes that were at their house. The island is only 18 kilometers long from north to south, and quite thinly stretched with one road down the middle. I don't remember seeing a car that day, just a few bikers like ourselves. We took the road going south as it has this beautiful hill at the end, called 'La Mola'. It was all straight until we got to the bottom of the hill, but then the road made its way up and up. Finally we got to 'El Mirador'. The view from up there was incredible and made the hardship of getting up there well worth it.

We could see over the whole island and its white sandy shores, as well as over to Ibiza in the distance. On the way back we passed by this old windmill where Bob Dylan had supposedly stayed at, though there is no written record to be found regarding that.

A bit tired from the bike-ride, I must have slept long because when I got up the next day the sun was already quite hot. I hadn't planned anything for today but felt that I needed to be alone. I wasn't expecting some huge breakthrough in my spiritual search, but if I was going to find any, I knew I was going to have to be alone. We often connect being alone with loneliness, so we tend to shy away from it, but sometimes it's good and necessary to be alone. It certainly turned out that way for me.

The island doesn't have very lush vegetation, so I wandered along past bushes and small fields with rocks surrounding them, and occasional small farmhouses, which seemed mostly abandoned. People had probably gone over to Ibiza where there was money to be made in tourism. The smell of all kinds of herbs mingled with the salty wind from the nearby sea, and I could hear some birds chirping loudly. The occasional hum of a bee or fly reminded me that I wasn't alone.

LONELY TRAVELLER

The fresh breeze from the sea invigorated my mind, and I took a deep breath of the herbal aroma, carried along by the wind from the small trees and the fields. The sun was shining down on me, I felt its warmth and I felt that today was going to be a step closer to what I was seeking. I had walked for about half an hour and found a lovely place along some stone wall, which someone must have built long ago. The sea wasn't far away as I could hear the waves splashing, but I didn't want to be distracted by the beauty of the sea which I love so much. But that stone wall looked like a very inviting place to sit down for some intensive time of meditation.

I don't know how long I'd been sitting down and meditating there when I felt like I heard this inner voice, one which put a soft wave of peace all over me. "There is peace to be found in the eternal now." I knew this wasn't my voice, as mine was filled with turmoil, and this voice gave me such inner peace. I was rejoicing inside that for the first time I had felt like I had really made some sort of a spiritual connection, and I felt extremely happy for the rest of the day. I thought that it had been worth travelling all the way to Formentera just to hear this one sentence. It was as if the sky, the clouds, the birds, the waves and the trees around me had all gathered together that day in order to give me that message.

Of course, they were probably speaking all the time, but for me it was the first time I had heard them to that extent. "There is peace to be found in the eternal now." I reflected on that for quite some time while just lying down in the grass and letting the sun caress me with its warm rays. Perhaps the 'eternal now' represents a place where one can retreat to from a life where one so often feels like being surrounded by problems and questions. A place where problems just become mere specks of dust, I was thinking.

I went back to the house, feeling quite encouraged and up-beat about my experience that day. The Dutch friends said that some hippies from England were organizing a party at the beach that night, with guitars and bongos, and quite a lot of people were going to come as news had spread at 'Fonda Pepe'. I felt like partying a bit that night and was looking forward to be among like-minded people.

The sun was going to set in about an hour when we got to the beach, and from afar we could hear drums and guitars and a flute, the all-familiar sound I love so much. I hadn't brought my bongos or guitar on this trip, but I had a new flute with me and was happy to join in. We didn't care much about perfection in those days, we were just jamming and I still love doing this in just the same way nowadays.

More hippies were streaming in and some brought wine, while others filled the air with some familiar smoke. When the sun finally set, there must have been around 50 people there. I was talking to Paul, telling him a bit about my experience I'd had that day. "That's amazing Bernardo, because today I also went out on my own after you had left, and I found this most beautiful spot and started drawing. I got so inspired and I think it's my favourite piece of art so far." I felt so thrilled for him. "I do hope you'll be able to develop your gift Paul, and that perhaps you'll be able to somehow make your living from it."

Paul was in thought for a moment. "You know, Bernardo, I think it's like this with creativity: I believe a lot more people would be creative if they'd have more time. It's this treadmill of an eight to five job that keeps people exhausted and unable to have any energy left to put their emotions and thoughts into something creative. I think one of the most important things you can do is to make sure you can allow yourself that freedom at some point in your life: to be creative."

"When you are creative it's your soul and your being that goes into whatever your creativity produces. If some people like it, that's just a pleasant addition, but not the main point. The main point is that you like it because it comes from inside of you and represents the real you."

"You seem to be into writing, Bernardo. I noticed you are writing quite a bit into that booklet you carry with you. Perhaps you should cultivate that too." He hit a certain point. I had wanted to become a journalist before and had actually visited a newspaper publisher. Of course, at that point no newspaper would have wanted to publish my critical views of society. And I wasn't to become some mainstream writer who just reflected what people are supposed to think in order to be considered 'normal'. "It's true Paul, I can write, but I lack insight and mostly spiritual experience. But I keep writing things down that I'm thinking about."

I had started jotting down notes on one of my trips to Amsterdam, mainly impressions, thoughts, but also questions about life that I wanted to find answers to. I was actually surprised that Paul had noticed, as I considered my time with my booklet somewhat 'holy'. Not even any of my girlfriends had found out about it.

I usually went for a few minutes to some quiet place if I felt there was something I needed to write down. That booklet had become an intricate part of my hippie-bag and I kept it like the apple of my eye.

During our conversation, I had noticed this beautiful girl sitting down not far from me. It looked as if she had come on her own, or was at least sitting on her own and not talking to anyone. There was a certain glow on her face, partly from the fire that had been lit in the meantime, but also from something else. There was a certain peaceful aura on her face that caught my attention. I kept observing her a while longer, while talking to Paul. She wore a long flowery skirt, dark blouse, and some kind of hair-band around her long brown hair, some of which was braided in the back. Her face seemed relaxed. She was listening to the music and her eyes were looking out to the sea into the distance.

"Paul, I think I'm going to go over to try to talk to that girl, she looks very interesting." I was generally quite an outgoing, social, and communicative person, but in moments like these I became very shy. So I took my flute and sat myself down behind her and started playing along with the rest of the music. It didn't take long for her to turn around, and this was the first time I saw her eyes. I swear at that moment I saw more stars in her eyes than there were up in the darkened sky.

I stopped playing my flute the moment she turned around as I felt so embarrassed. "Don't stop playing, it's so beautiful", she said with a big smile. Her smile made the night look like the brightest of sunny days. "Good vibrations here", I said. It's a miracle that even this short comment found its way out of my mouth as I felt almost speechless. I felt quite relieved that I had said at least something halfway significant at that moment.

"My name is Anne. Nice to meet you", she said with a French accent. "My name's Bernardo and we can speak in French if you prefer." I was used to it, coming from a bilingual city, though my first language was German. As it turned out, Anne originated from a village not far from where I came from, and her father was of Swiss-German, and her mom of Swiss-French origin. She had grown up with both languages. "Do you sometimes visit my home-town?" I was wondering why I had never seen her before. "I needed to go there sometimes, but I've been living here for a year already. My boyfriend's a painter, and he paints and I sell his paintings for him. I had also spent a few months on Ibiza before that, so I haven't been back to Switzerland for quite a while." Now I understood why I hadn't seen her before.

"It's interesting how you can stay here on this island with sand and sea and make a living. I will need to go back soon as I don't have much money." She explained how it actually went quite well for them with selling the paintings, and that she would sometimes go over to Ibiza and sell them there as well. 'He must be a lucky man', I thought, 'doing his hobby while his beautiful girlfriend sells his paintings.' "You should talk to my friend Paul over there, he would like to live from selling his paintings as well. As for me, I'm not that creative. I will probably end up at some factory-job for a while when I get back." She looked at me with those warm eyes. "You can't do anything else?"

she asked. "Well, I finished commercial school, but I'm not going into the economy. I started disliking society and its materialistic treadmill, so right now I'm trying to spend as little of my time in it as I can. Just enough to make a little bit of money, so that I can continue travelling and finding out what I'm supposed to do in this world", I said. "I know how difficult it is to find the right thing to do", she said. "I had studied tourism. My parents wanted me to do so in order to eventually work in their business. They're running a hotel with a restaurant up in the 'Jura Mountains'." I loved that area, and often went there hiking with friends. That mountain range began right above my hometown and stretched from there way over to France.

"I just couldn't take it anymore and so I stopped", she continued; "I am more of a creative type of person and that's more my world. Besides, I became a hippie when I was seventeen and started questioning every-thing." So she must be about my age, I thought. "Like a rolling stone?" It sort of slipped out of my mouth. "Exactly, Bernardo, like a rolling stone, that's how it felt at first. In the meantime, thanks to the distance from it all, I feel that I've become more peaceful inside. The sun and the sea have done me a lot of good. I have even started creating some things myself."

"Really, like what?" It sounded great and I wanted to hear more. "I make bracelets and necklaces. I haven't had the courage to sell them yet, but I'm con-sidering it. It's just that Pierre's paintings sell quite well and we can live from it. If I weren't selling them for him, he might not sell any, as he isn't good at sell-ing." I smiled: "I can understand that, I don't think I'd be good at selling either."

43

"I will go back in a week or so, and I don't know where to go on from there, maybe to India," I continued. "You seem to be really searching, Bernardo" she replied. "I am". – "So was I, but I have found a lot during my time here. I've made a few spiritual experiences that have had quite an impact on me. I will stay for now; Pierre needs me, and it's sort of benefitting the both of us for the time being."

"My stay here has helped me too, and just today I had a very special experience," and I told her all about it. "That sounds great, Bernardo. There are indeed voices to be heard; in the waves, from the trees, from the stars and the sun. Taking distance from the busy world does really help one to open up to what they're trying to tell us." She seemed wise and like she had already somewhat acquired what I had just gotten into.

We kept talking for quite a while longer and it seemed we had forgotten time. "I think I should be getting back to Pierre now, maybe I will be here tomorrow night again in case you'd want to talk some more." – "That would be great; it was lovely talking to you, Anne." Then she turned around, and looked at me and I felt like streams of warm energy flowing from her eyes. With a soothing and at the same time steady voice she said: "Bernardo, I think there are basically three kinds of people: There are those who are not seeking, at least not knowingly, and living off material things, which brings them a certain satisfaction. Then there are others, like you, who are seeking for more. And yet others who have found through their seeking, but even they should never stop seeking." This woman was full of wisdom. For a moment I thought I must have met my guru.

Anne came the next two nights as well, and we continued to have deep conversations. We were talking about different religions and their spiritual value. "Anne, I've read a lot over these past years from all kinds of sources. And I think that people like Jesus and Buddha and others had a lot of important things to tell us. Just before coming here I had been reading the New Testament, and I believe in the things Jesus said, many hippies do. I also read a lot from Buddha and also in the Bhagavad Gita. "Perhaps there are things to extract everywhere," she said, "but in the end it's your own spiritual experiences that will get you somewhere."

"Anne, do you think I would find more answers if I went to India and Nepal?" She thought for a moment. "I think you will find it in time, Bernardo. And that's much less dependent on a location than on your inner desperation and receptivity."

The next three nights she didn't show up. I spent my time talking to other people and Paul always came with me as well. We didn't always talk as sometimes he'd work on his sunset drawings. During daytime I went to check out the schedules for the boat and the ferry in order to get back to the mainland. There was one leaving from Ibiza to Valencia in a couple of days so I decided I was going to take that one. I had been on a short trip to Gandia a couple summers before with a friend of mine, and I wanted to pass by and see if any of my friends happened to be there.

My last night at the beach, I could finally see Anne walking over the small hill that was overlooking the ocean... She looked gorgeous and I felt very excited to see her. "I'm sorry I couldn't come the last few nights," she said. "We ran out of money and I needed to go to Ibiza and sell some paintings there." I told her that she made it just on time, as I was going to leave the next day. "I felt like we could talk very openly, and I want to get close to other people besides my boyfriend. I don't mean sexually, but I need more friends," she said. "And I felt that you have a good heart, Bernardo, and that you are sincere, and that's what I like about you." I told her that I had also really enjoyed talking to her and was happy she had come back one more time just before I was going to leave.

"Look, Anne, you're basically standing in front of a very lonely traveller. My search is a lonely one; I have lots of friends, but no one who is really close to me. Perhaps I have a hard time really trusting people. I had been hurt really badly by some people who had led me into a bad trip up in Holland." - "I can understand that, Bernardo. We were like innocent children, always thinking that people were going to be good to us, and we trusted everyone. But then we grew up and realized there was so much mischief in this world. It came to the point where we even needed to learn to mistrust people. It's crazy!"

"Anne, I'm also really having a problem seeing where this world is going to. I love nature, I love the animals, but it's slowly getting destroyed by the tremendous industrialization that is taking place, and this saddens me. Where is this world heading to, and is anyone able to stop this madness?"

Anne was looking out towards the sea, maybe it was a big wave that had caught her attention, or maybe that's what she did when she was deep in thought. Then she looked at me, and I knew I could expect some wise words just from the look and expression on her face and the passion in her eyes: "All the different resources mother earth has, some deep down below the earth, have become such a matter of greed among mankind to where they fight wars over them. It will always be very difficult for me to understand why people can be so irresponsible as to abuse mother earth continuously, thinking that she won't tire out one day and stop giving mankind even our basic needs."

"Well, Anne, it almost makes me not want to be a part of this world, really. That's why I'm a hippie; I feel at least I'm being a part of a whole lot of people who also don't want to be part of this madness. But I'm searching, and I don't know if I'll find something better." - "Bernardo, your search is not going to be in vain. Don't get discouraged by all you see and how you feel about the world. You won't be able to change much, but you can change inside to where you become those things you wish to see."

We exchanged warm hugs, as well as our addresses for writing, and decided to stay in touch. "If you really search for it you will find it, Bernardo," were the last words she said to me, as she disappeared over the hill. I was left with a mix of excitement to have met such a wonderful woman, but also with a bit of sadness. We had gotten so close in our deep conversations and I had really enjoyed being with her.

Eclipse Of The Soul

The next morning I left quite early to catch the boat to Ibiza, after bidding farewell to the hippies I had been staying with, including Paul. From Ibiza I caught the ferry over to Valencia and continued hitchhiking to Gandia, where I went directly to the place where my friends would usually hang out at that hour. Sure enough, some of them were there. One of them was going to go back to Switzerland in a couple of days on his Vespa roller. He offered me to get on the back and travel with him. I felt that would be great as I just wanted to get back home to my room at the hippie-commune, and sort out all my new impressions and thoughts.

One of the first things I found out after getting back to our hippie-commune was that Carol had gotten involved with one of my friends. We did talk about it a couple of days later and she explained to me that she felt more secure now in her new relationship, as with me she could feel that I was restless and searching. She was right.

My inner search started intensifying. I didn't go around anymore to every 'smoke' in town. I started going more often my own way. My friends of course all wanted to know how it was on Formentera, and I shared some of the experiences with them. It was always fun when one of us came back from a trip and shared all that had happened. There was no internet in those days and very little film or photo material about those places, so one had to gather his information directly in person.

It's a fact that the hippies used to live quite primitively in comparison with today's youth. We had no mobile phones, no computers and internet, could hardly afford a good camera; that's why there are so few pictures from the 60's and 70's. We practically couldn't afford those horrendous plane fares which in those days seemed to be only affordable for the wealthy. So hitchhiking wasn't just a 'cool thing' to do, although many of us looked at it that way, but it was also due to economic reasons, as most of us hippies were actually very poor.

After somewhat settling into my life back home, I found some work helping to build a house. There were only three of us building it, but since one of us knew what to do, he only needed two helpers. So there were the two of us hippies helping this professional builder. Sometimes after work, the other hippie and I used to go smoke a joint. It was sort of cool to work with a buddy who was into similar things I was, it made work somewhat easier. It wasn't a big house we were building, so we could see day by day some progress, and in the process I learned a lot about construction. It was hard work too, but it helped me realize that things that were supposed to last a bit needed to be built step-by-step, making sure everything is done well in order to ensure good quality.

LONELY TRAVELLER

I spent my free time going to the 'Ashram' to meditate, or down to the lake to watch the sunset with the other hippies. It was autumn now; summer was over, and I felt that spiritually I was going into a bit of a winter sleep. At that time I wasn't so much into winter anymore and longed for the warm sun and the beaches. It was time to put on my Afghan sheep coat again as the days were getting colder.

Sometimes I felt like that coat was the only thing I still liked about winter. Though when winter came, we did take some beautiful walks up in the snow-covered mountains of the 'Jura', and we usually went into one of those mountain-inns to have a special coffee. It had some spirits in it which really warmed me up from the inside. Or sometimes we'd even have a 'Fondue' (melted cheese in hot white wine).

I had to take on another job, as the job in construction had been put on hold. It was getting too cold to work outside. I ended up taking a job at a watch factory where all completed watches had to be put to the right time. So I had this master-clock in front of me to which all watches needed to be synchronized to, hundreds of them a day. This master-clock had a second hand, so I could literally count the seconds and see my life ticking away.

Winter was hard and somewhat boring, but I really wanted to make some money to get out of there and go to India. I would often think about Anne and our conversations and how much I'd been able to take in from her. She had sent me a postcard from Formentera. "The summer's gone; so are you, but you're still in my thoughts and prayers." Thinking about her made me both sad and happy. Sad because I missed having someone like her around, but happy for her, that she could be in Formentera enjoying the warm sun. How lucky her boyfriend was to not only have Anne as a companion, but also to be able to paint and sell his paintings, and make a living that way. Here I was, working at a job where I was literally counting the seconds.

Spring Awakening

After a few weeks, just before going mad, I found another job cleaning windows, which was a bit more enjoyable as one could always look out and see the sights. But all in all it was a difficult and somewhat lonely winter, and I was so much looking forward to spring. It wasn't clear to me what I was going to do then, but just the thought of spring alone brought on some new hope.

I had always loved springtime so much. As temperatures would slowly be rising again, I could see the first tiny little buds on the trees, and hear the first few birds slowly daring to chirp a little song of hope that spring might be here soon. They always brought such joy and anticipation to my heart as spring is sort of an equivalent for the warmer days ahead, spiritually too. The first snowdrops took the risk of cautiously opening their white petals to the first rays of sunshine, hoping they would somehow survive the cold nights, while other spring flowers were still struggling to push their way through the earth in order to come out and see what was going on.

There were some cooler days in between again, but on the days when the sun came out, the intensity of excitement grew each time. It wasn't long until the first butterfly was chasing after the sun's rays to keep itself warm. With each sunny day the irresistible desire for change and freedom seemed to grow, and it didn't take long for all this yearning of nature to climax in a mighty explosion of thousands of birds singing, accompanied by white, yellow, pink, and a diversity of green blossoms bursting out of the trees. At the same time, all kinds of flowers with psychedelic colors were popping out everywhere so that mother earth would be covered and adorned with an incredible beauty. Oh, if only there was such a spiritual awakening among mankind as well!

It was around Easter that along with more sun, more and more hippies would come down to the lake again, play the guitar, smoke a joint and talk about life. The 'normal' people would walk by and look at us like we'd be some kind of animals in a zoo. The two worlds just didn't seem to jive. I still visited my parents sometimes, but it was always hard, as I could see them struggle due to their worries about my future, and what I was going to do. I felt sorry for them, but just had to follow that voice in my heart, and there was nobody that would have been able to stop me from doing so.

I started having a little bit of money aside from the jobs I had done during the winter, but no idea where to go or what to do. The thought of going to India, Nepal, or Afghanistan kept going through my mind, but at that point none of my friends were interested in going with me, nor had the money. I didn't have much either, and was thinking that for going on such a long journey I would need quite a bit more and perhaps also some extra to allow me to come back, in case I wouldn't find there what I would be looking for. Somewhere in my heart I felt that it wasn't the right time for me to go there.

One of the early summer weekends some of my friends and I took our sleeping bags and some food and went to the top of 'Mont Soleil' (Sun Mountain) in order to spend the night there. That mountain towered high above our city and the lake. From the top you could see all the way across the rolling hills and farm-land until the Alps. Most likely, this mountain may have received its name because of the fabulous sun-sets, and it had truly been worth the climb to watch the sun slowly set behind the lake in the distance. I was thinking about how much a sunset takes us into its grip, no matter where it happens; it's an amazing thing. The warmest of colors can be seen just when the sun is close to setting, and the different shimmers of red and orange would remain on the horizon for a long time after the sun itself had disappeared.

We had some very good discussions about life that night around the fire. My friend Robert, who lived next door at our hippie-commune, was there as well. I had been having quite a few good talks with him lately. We would often walk to the lake together and then have discussions way into the night. What I ap-preciated about him too was the fact that he was al-ways helping to keep the kitchen clean. I liked people, who took on their share of the load, which I thought was an important point when living in a hippie-com-munity.

He understood my search, though he himself seemed much more settled and knew what he wanted to do. "Bernardo, I do understand your desire to go to India; a lot of hippies are going there these days. But you also need to realize that you might not find there what you're seeking. I think for you it seems to be more of a matter of finding the right thing to believe in and what to do with your life, and not so much finding the right place." I felt he had a point, and Anne had mentioned something similar when I had asked her about this topic.

The sun had left its glow, leaving a shimmer of red and pinkish light on the snow-covered Alps in the distance. We eventually got tired and lay down in our sleeping bags. I felt very restless that night and wasn't able to sleep. These big questions about my life were haunting me, and I felt I needed to get a grip on something in this restless sea of waves. So I just got up and walked the few meters to the very top and began to meditate and pray, more seriously than ever before. I remembered what Anne had told me when I last saw her: "If you really search for it you will find it."

I was trying hard to shut out all my thoughts and hear that still small voice again. And there it was: "Seek, and you will find; knock and it will be opened unto you." That sounded pretty good. Hadn't I read something similar in the 'New Testament' a while back? Perhaps it was the same thing, I could check that later.

Mind you, I had read a lot of books about spiritual things from different religions, including the 'New Testament'. I had various Christian groups trying to convert me, but I had always told them that I already believed in Jesus. "He was a hippie too", I used to tell them. "He was so high that maybe he didn't need to smoke weed." You should have seen their faces. They understood me as little as I understood them, and I hadn't found my 'home' with them, as you can imagine. I had noticed too much of a negative view on hippies, whereas I thought that one of the strong points the hippies had was their tolerance, which seemed more in line with what I had read about Jesus. But apart from not being very turned on by the groups I'd met or even visited, I had nothing against Jesus and the things he had said and done. I might want to ask him one day about a couple things, and I'm sure he will explain them to me.

So I was very encouraged by this voice I had just heard from the stars above, or maybe from the moon that was shining in almost full appearance over the lake, or from anywhere within or without. It didn't matter to me from where, but I'd heard it. "Seek, and you will find; knock and it will be opened unto you." "If this is so, then please just help me and show me!" I screamed out into the darkened sky. Don't know if any of my friends, who were asleep, heard it or not. Maybe not, because I had gone up to this little ledge on top of the mountain to meditate.

It didn't take longer than a second after my shout of desperation that everything around turned into light and warm energy, like someone would have turned on a light-switch in a dark room. From one moment to the next, the trees and each blade of grass were emitting warmth and the most beautiful shining colors of light. At first I didn't know if I should be scared or not, as I'd never experienced something like this before, not even on my wildest drug-trips. I thought: "Why should I be scared, it's so beautiful, and I've asked for it." And you should have seen the sky: There was so much light up there that I couldn't even see the stars anymore, with beams of light streaming down.

A tremendous inner peace came over me along with the feeling of assurance that I was in good hands, and that everything was going to be okay. I wasn't scared, even though I couldn't feel my body anymore; it was like my own spirit had gone out and was becoming a part of everything around me, part of that warmth and light. I did do some intensive thinking too while all this was happening. Apart from absorbing all those wonderful feelings and intensive energy, the thought came to me: 'The power behind everything we see in nature is love, and I am a part of the same'. Somehow, maybe because of the desperation in my quest over the last years, my cry out into the dark had been answered. I felt I had found something major that would forever serve as a reference point in my life from now on.

I have heard and read from various people since then who had similar spiritual experiences. This was of course life-changing for me, and I knew I had gotten ahold of something that was much deeper than any concept of Heaven I'd been taught as a child, or at school or thereafter. I couldn't even integrate that experience into any religious or non-religious concept at all. I have developed a great respect and love for nature and this loving spiritual power that surrounds us. I prefer to think of it as spiritual energy, while others prefer to call it God. But the word God has this sort of connotation of an old man with a long grey beard, and I hadn't experienced it like that at all. I have gained great respect for people who made similar spiritual experiences, no matter from which background or religion they come from.

The morning following this experience, my friends wanted to go back to town, as such a night up on top of the mountain called for some kind of hearty breakfast. Personally, I was apprehensive of going back to the city, even though I was hungry too. I just felt so scared of losing this new found feeling and spiritual contact I had made up there. Somehow I felt that there would be no easier place to lose this again than down in the busy confusion. But I realized I needed to go get some food too, as I was not at a stage in my life where I could just stay up there and live off of berries and mushrooms. So despite it being hard to go back to town, I just had to have the trust that I would somehow be able to retain as much of what I had found.

Life went on. I went back to work, whatever sort of work came up, to make some money. I worked at a great variety of jobs as they were only temporary assignments. This was good for me as I could sometimes take a break in between one job and the next. At that point I was once again seriously considering getting ready to go to India, in hopes of finding some place that would allow me to stay in that spiritual state I had found. Perhaps to some 'Ashram', far away from civilization, where I could just offer my help and labor in the field without needing to go work for money. But until then I would need to continue acquiring quite a bit more for such a trip.

Besides working, I continued with meditation and prayer in order to stay as close as possible to this experience I'd had. It was difficult, as the daily humdrum was cutting out so much of this, and coming home tired from a nine-hour job didn't exactly help either. 'Why would people need to work so much', I asked myself. 'Some people are out of work, so why don't we just work less and give others an opportunity, while we have more time for meditation, prayer, for being creative and most of all, for talking to each other!'

I spent the week working and at the weekend I would often go to one of the autonomous youth-centers which some of the cities around had established for their hippies. 'Autonomous' meant these places were run by young people and that there were no police raids there, and that we could listen to music as loud as we wanted, and no one cared about where all the smoke in there came from.

During that time, my intake of drugs was diminishing considerably. I felt like I had gone much higher than the psychedelic state some of the drugs had taken me to, and that it was becoming a waste to fill myself with more drugs. I still smoked occasionally but would stay away from the stronger stuff I'd taken many times before. I felt those drugs wouldn't bring me to any higher state than the one I'd already found.

Drugs were a major part of the hippie-lifestyle, and for many it wasn't just a new way to escape, like society at large has done for centuries with alcohol. It was part of our spiritual search into our souls, and what one wanted to live for and why we're here. I'm not saying that drugs need to be part of such a spiritual search. I'm just saying that many hippies tried them out as part of their spiritual search, including myself. Since I don't want to be known for misleading people into using drugs I won't elaborate on it any further. I've seen too many young hippies getting into ad-

dictive drugs, and whenever I would see them inject-
ing a needle with heroin or opium into their veins, I always felt very sad that they had decided to slowly end
their lives, instead of searching for a better world.

A Ray Of Hope

I had written Anne a letter, informing her of my work, and my saving up money to go to India. And I actually wrote her that it's difficult to find a woman like her; I was surprised at myself how much I opened up to her. Then one day I received a letter that was sent from her parent's place. She wrote me that she had returned home after breaking up with Pierre. She mentioned something about having stayed with a hippie-commune in the 'Jura' for two weeks, to sort things out in her mind. Now she had started work at a watch factory and would be looking forward to meeting me. That was certainly news that hit me like a lightening from the sky! When I called her parents' place, she wasn't in. Her mother said she would let her know that I had called.

Like most evenings after work, I decided to go down to the lake. It was a beautiful early summer evening, and I thought I would watch the sunset. Some of my friends were there too, and we watched the sunset together. Once again I got this peaceful feeling that everything was going to be well. I had been there for about half an hour when suddenly I heard a voice behind me: "Bernardo, is that you?" I turned around and there she was: Even lovelier than when I had last seen her on Formentera. "Anne...I can't believe this, what are you doing here?" We hugged for a long time. "It's a complicated story Bernardo....", and she started filling me in on how Pierre had found another woman, and she had moved out. She had no more money to stay on Formentera, so she had returned home.

After work she had decided to come to town to see if she would find me. I could not only see a reflection of the sunset in her dark-brown eyes, but also a certain pain and sadness. "Sorry to hear about Pierre" I said. "It's best like that," she replied, "because it had been a relationship that was partly based on convenience, as I was able to sell his paintings and so he supported me. I didn't have to worry about money. I don't know what to do next, but I don't want to stay here. My parents would be happy if I'd work in their business, but I don't feel called to do that."

"I had been contemplating to visit you at your address", she said. "But then I decided to come down here to the lake in hopes that I might find you here, watching the sunset." I was just thrilled to see her again. She went on to explain that after she had come back a few weeks ago, she had gotten involved with a Christian type of hippie-commune near where she lived. One of her friends who had been heavily involved with drugs had gone there, and it seemed to have helped her somewhat. Anne felt a situation like that might help her sort things out after her break-up with Pierre. She had actually moved there for a couple of weeks. "They had some kind of a leader or guru, and many of the things he said were quite wise," she said. "But I noticed that everyone there had made him the center of everything and all the rules for this community were made by him. Then one day I was listening to my 'Cat Stevens' record and one of the staff came and asked me to turn it off because they didn't listen to hippie music anymore. Well, Bernardo, as you can imagine, that was the end of my stay there." I was glad to hear that. "I did learn some useful things about prayer though, and some of the people there were really nice. Maybe for some, especially for those trying to get away from drug-addiction, it seemed to be important to have a regulated lifestyle for a while. I was just crushed after coming back, because of this thing with Pierre, and thought that staying with this community might help me."

She needed to catch the last train, but we agreed to meet next weekend at the youth center. "It was so good to see you again, Bernardo. We must see each other more." That was my idea too. I don't know what it was about Anne, but I felt such a warm feeling when meeting her again. I felt sad that she had gone through these sad experiences, but at the same time I was also glad she was around. I was really looking forward to more time to talk and share more about the experiences we'd had.

I went to the youth center the next weekend. Some of my friends were there too, but this time I wasn't looking for them. My heart jumped when I saw her dancing. I had never seen her dance before and my eyes were glued to her. There was an air of freedom in the way she moved her body; so sexy, yet not trying to impress, but just moving with the emotions of the music and expressing them through her body. I must have been watching her for about ten minutes, when the song ended and she went over to talk to some friends. But I could see she was looking around, probably for me. When she saw me her eyes lit up and she came running right across the room and hugged me warmly. "Bernardo...so nice you came. I wanted to see you. I have lots to tell you."

We went to get ourselves a drink. "I realize that you had some heartbreaking experiences, Anne." She looked at me and I could see a moment of appreciation. "Yes, Bernardo, it wasn't easy. I hadn't planned on coming back; I would have preferred to stay on Formentera. But after what had happened, I just wanted to get away from Pierre and the situation. Now I just need time to see what I'm going to do next."

I started explaining to her about my experience up on 'Mont Soleil' a few weeks before. "This is just amazing, Bernardo. I just knew you would find it, because you were searching so hard for it."

She had so much light in her eyes when she was excited about something. "Yes, Anne, what you had told me was true, and I did really search for it. But I also know I need to keep searching for it, because the connection weakens at times with all the daily affairs going on." She replied: "I know, Bernardo. Right now I'm also a bit under all kinds of influences which make it rather difficult to keep that contact."

It was amazing. She felt quite similar on so many issues. I had already felt very attracted to her before while she was still with Pierre, and now she was suddenly alone. That was a whole new ballgame. I wasn't eager to jump into a relationship though, and she didn't seem to either. I wanted to concentrate on my spiritual link I had found, and if anything was going to work out in terms of a relationship, I was going to just let it come to me without pushing for it. But I really liked Anne!

It was getting quite late and Anne mentioned she would need to take the last train as otherwise she'd need to wait for the first one in the morning. I offered her to sleep at my place. "Okay, but just to sleep," she said, as she gave me a warm smile. "You're going to meet Alice", I said. She looked at me in surprise and I explained to her that Alice was my cat I'd gotten a few months ago. "You have a cat, Bernardo? I love cats and can't wait to see her."

So she was of course on cloud seven to meet Alice and I showed her around my place and the hippie-commune, as we went around looking for whoever was still awake. I put on a candle and some incense, accompanied by some Pink Floyd. I let her sleep on my bed, while I slept on my thick floor cushions which were almost like a bed too, with Alice next to me. We kept talking for another hour or so until we fell asleep. I remember thinking, just before drifting off, how I was so thankful that destiny had brought us back together again.

The next morning I was up first and went to the kitchen, where I found Robert already up. We had a coffee together and he told me he also had a young lady visiting in his room who was still asleep. So we decided to bring them each a coffee with some fresh croissants from the bakery nearby. Anne was so excited about it. "That's so sweet of you, Bernardo. I totally enjoy waking up like that!" It sure felt good to be so appreciated. 'Appreciation', I thought. How many people don't feel appreciated in this world? Who is

there standing at the door of a factory and telling people after a hard day's work: "Thank you!"

Quo Vadis

We started spending as much of our free time together as we could. Anne was still working at the watch factory. Being able to meet for the weekends made our time at work more bearable. I had no phone at our hippie commune, but her parents had one, so sometimes I would call her. Her mom answered the phone one evening and said that Anne had been talking to her about me, and that she would like to invite me over to get to know me. So a couple evenings later I went there, and Anne came with her mom to pick me up at the train station and they drove me to their house. We had a very good conversation that night, and I realized that Anne's mom was actually a very understanding woman. "I know Anne doesn't want to help to take over the family business. Her brother can do that. I just want Anne to be happy and find what she is looking for." It's nice to have parents supporting you in your search, I thought.

Next time I met Anne, she was all excited about some news from her friend Jaqueline, who had just returned from travelling Europe for a while. Apparently, she had ended up on the island of La Gomera, and had told Anne how beautiful it was there, and that quite a number of hippies were moving to a place called Valle Gran Rey (Valley of the Great King). So we looked it up on a map and found out that this island was situated at the most south-western tip of Europe. It is one of the Canary Islands out in the Atlantic Ocean, off the coast of North Africa.

"Jaqueline said she had taken a ferry from Cadiz to Las Palmas first, and then went on with some other ferries to Tenerife and finally on to La Gomera." Well, it sure seemed that someone had put a bug into Anne's ear; she seemed to be really excited about it. "She explained that she had met hippies there who were selling bracelets and self-made stuff to the tourists and they were able to live from that. I could try that too," she said with sparkling eyes. It seemed like once she had gotten excited about something, nothing could stop her. I had never heard of hippies living on La Gomera. I had actually never heard much about the Canary Islands at all. "It sure is far away from Europe", I said. "I'd like to find out more about it."

The Canary Islands: I started reading about them at the library and at travel agencies, but could find very little about La Gomera. It is part of a group of seven islands off the coast of Africa, but belongs to Spain. Some of the other places there seemed to be very touristic, but La Gomera hadn't been developed by the tourist industry. It had a beautiful rainforest though and the inhabitants were living off of fishing and agriculture.

"I speak Spanish, I've learned it quite well during my long stay on Formentera", Anne said. "I speak some too", I told her and smiled: "I just mix my French with my Italian." I had been good at languages at school. I had learned French from an early age and English hadn't been a problem either, and later on I had also joined a course in Italian.

I visited Carlos at one of the hippie shops in town. He always seemed to know all kinds of things, and when people needed a ride somewhere he would always let them put up little notes in his shop. He had been to places like Nepal, India and Morocco, and had always brought some things back that he would sell in his shop. Things like oriental lamps, and all kinds of drapes and pipes and hand-made jewelry. He was not just running a shop; he was sort of the hippie communication-center in our area. He always knew which band would come to give a concert, and his entrance door was always full of advertisement of the hippie festivals taking place. Being quite an intellectual guy he was always reading up on various hippie-related news, and if anybody in town would know anything about La Gomera, it would certainly be him.

He was gay, and it seemed he was a bit after me. Since I personally wasn't inclined to be gay, I had to disappoint him once in his attempts, but I still kept going to his shop sometimes. To me his ideology, kindness, and tolerance were more important than his gender-preferences. That's how I generally kept it with guys that were after me, there were actually quite a few. I always got along fine with them without getting sexually involved.

"Carlos, have you heard anything about La Gomera lately? I heard it's a new hippie-hangout." He looked at me sort of like 'where do you know that from'. He was usually always the first one who would know things like that. "You heard it right, Bernardo.

Valle Gran Rey on La Gomera was first discovered by some American and Canadian hippies, but in the meantime hippies from all over Europe have been streaming there, mainly a lot of German hippies." I was not surprised he knew all about it. "I guess I haven't been to Amsterdam for a while, I would have probably heard about it there. Thanks for the info, I'm trying to find out more about it", I told him.

I had already mentioned to him before about my trip to Formentera. "From what I know it's another place somewhat similar to Formentera, a place where mass tourism hasn't put its imprints yet", he added. "You need to go through the island of Tenerife if you want to get there. Tenerife is very touristic and lots of planes fly there from Europe."

So that's how I found more information about this place, La Gomera, and I told Anne. She was eager to go soon. "I just don't want to stay here much longer; it's too busy around here. The first days after coming back from Formentera, I felt like I had landed in New York, life is just so hectic here." I could relate to that, and that was one reason I had been preparing and setting money aside to leave again. "It's true, Anne. It's difficult to concentrate and meditate and pray in such a busy world. Perhaps one day, when one is really used to it and has a really strong connection, it might be easier to live in the midst of a stressed-out society. But I definitely want to get away and go somewhere I can strengthen the connections I've found, somewhere quiet."

"I'm going to find out as much as I can from Jaqueline, about where to land, where to sleep and where to eat and so on." We hadn't been talking at all about going anywhere together, but perhaps we already felt that something was taking shape, as we kept talking about it quite often when meeting each other. Anne had started doing yoga and went regularly to a yoga teacher in her village. "I want to learn different things, Bernardo, perhaps one day I can make money with it. And doing yoga has really helped me to concentrate on something else than just my problems."

I thought that it wouldn't be bad to learn some trade to make some money with while enjoying it at the same time. I just hadn't noticed any big talent in my life so far. I had started playing the guitar, and had learned some basic songs like "Blowing in the wind "and "Peace train", some songs with simple cords. I could sing and had some experience from the band, but I just hadn't been into it enough to make a living from it. "Yes, maybe one day you can live from making your bracelets, or from becoming a yoga teacher", I told Anne.

She was learning her yoga fast. Her body was very flexible too. Each time she would visit me at my place she would show me some new position she had learned. "I'm practicing daily, but I'm combining it with meditation. I get much more out of it that way", she said. I hadn't been much into yoga; I was more into meditation. "I could learn a couple new positions from you as well", I suggested. I was glad she had found something that seemed to add to her spiritual well-being, and she seemed to be more challenged and hopeful since she had started doing yoga. "My yoga teacher said that I make more progress than anyone she's known, and I was very happy to hear that." She was just amazing, as anything she put her heart into seemed to just flourish.

It was a warm summer in every way. Meeting Anne regularly had brought fresh colour into my life and though we hadn't gotten romantic, it was a very special friendship that was growing each time we met. Anne had gotten to know everyone at the hippie-commune where I was living and my friends became her friends. We'd all go out on sunny weekends and spend the day somewhere by the lake, playing the guitar, reading and talking and just having a relaxing time, as during the week we were both working. I'd gotten to know Anne's friend Jaqueline as well. She had started setting money aside to travel to India with another friend.

Anne would usually spend the weekend sleeping at my place and we'd often talk way into the night about our thoughts and dreams. "When the summer's over, I'd like to go, Bernardo", she said on one such occasion. "I want the summer to go on, but since it doesn't continue here, I want to go where it does." I felt like that too. She turned around and looked straight into my eyes: "Let's get out of here together, Bernardo. We can go to La Gomera; we already know a few things about that place. I want to go travel with you; I don't know anyone I'd like to go more with than you." Wow, that was almost half a declaration of love, I thought. "I think I could create and sell jewelry there, I do already speak quite a bit of Spanish. I personally don't feel led to go to India. But most important: I want to go with you!"

I did have this thought going through my mind that it's more important who you travel with than where you travel. "I would love to go with you, Anne; we've become such close friends." -"Bernardo, I'm sure we will make it somehow, maybe we can find a way to support ourselves there!" I liked her hopeful and positive attitude, but added that perhaps we could take some time to meditate and pray and see if we get any spiritual hint about this trip. I guess I just wanted to make sure I wasn't going to lose any of the spiritual connection I had gained by going off somewhere I was not supposed to go.

So the next day we went down to the lake for sunset, climbed up the cliff-road to find ourselves a quiet place and sat down together for meditation and prayer. We sat quietly and both really wanting to hear some clues to whether we were going the right direction or not. I had still India in the back of my mind, but then again I felt that Anne was very excited about going to La Gomera ever since Jaqueline had told her about it. I would love to go travelling with her and being with her every day instead of only at the weekends. Then I tried to just shut out all these thoughts. "Go where the doors are open for you." I could hear that still small voice again and it was not only very comforting, I felt I could count on it and that if I followed it, things would work out just fine.

We must have sat there in silence for quite some time, because the sun had set in the meantime, and Anne said: "It's getting a bit cold." I looked at her and wondered if she had gotten anything out of this meditation time. "I didn't hear anything in particular, Bernardo, but I just strongly feel we should go where the doors are open." She looked a bit sad. "I just don't want to keep you from going to India if you feel in your heart that you need to go there."

My heart was so touched that she really cared. "We're going together, because I got the exact same thing you did, to 'go where the doors are open for you.'" Her eyes lit up after I said that and she just turned around and gave me this big hug and was almost screaming for joy. I really liked these spontaneous outbreaks of her emotions. "I don't think this is a co-incidence that we both got the same thing, Anne. We do seem to have enough money to go to La Gomera, for going to India we would need quite a bit more, which might take another few months of staying here. But it's time to go where the doors are open." Anne didn't say anything, she just smiled and put her head on my shoulder as we were walking back, and she had that peaceful expression on her face which made her look so extremely beautiful.

The next week we started tying up loose ends. I needed to get my name off the contract and turn over my room to someone else, as I didn't want to keep paying rent, not knowing if and when I would return. We visited Anne's mom one more time. She was very open about it: "I felt for a while that Anne needs to go again, and I am happy to know that she is going with you, Bernardo. I feel like she's in good hands." My parents were a little more concerned, they would have preferred me getting back to some professional aspirations. But they did like meeting Anne and she seemed to leave quite a good impression with them. I had reassured them that I was going to stay in touch and call once we would get there.

I stopped by Carlos's shop a few times just to see if anyone would be driving down to Spain. And sure enough, a couple would be going down to Barcelona in about a week's time and would be able to take two people along, expecting a contribution towards the gasoline expenses. I called them up and they were very happy to take us along. I'd found out that flights to Tenerife were a lot cheaper from Barcelona than from Switzerland and I told Anne about it. "See how everything is working out when we follow those inner voices?" She was just thrilled.

Anne spent the night at my place before leaving. We had a little goodbye party with my friends. The girl that was taking over my room and signing the rental contract was there too, her name was Monica. She had bought my stereo and record collection, my guitar and bongos, and I left her my few pieces of furniture which I had bought at the flea-market, and some dishes in the kitchen. She was also going to care for my cat Alice. Robert had also offered to take care of my cat; she had gotten used to be in and out of his room as he had a cat as well. The two cats were actually brother and sister; we had gotten them together from the same farmer. They do say that cats get more attached to places instead of people, so I was hoping that this was true. It wasn't easy to leave Alice, as she had always been anxiously waiting for me to come back when I needed to go somewhere.

Monica seemed very happy for us. "I'd love to go travel like that too, but I feel like I'd want to find the right person to go with first, that would make a big difference," she said. "I think it does, and I'm happy that I found such a lovely friend to go with", I replied while looking over to Anne who was smiling. Robert was a bit sad that I left, but apparently he got along quite well with Monica who was now moving in next to him, and the night before she had slept at his place. "I wish both of you the best for this adventure", he said with a bit of sadness." My only comfort is that I'm getting a very pleasant replacement in the room next to mine". This time it was Monica who smiled. "We promise to take good care of Alice." We agreed to stay in touch through the mail.

The next morning the couple driving to Barcelona came to pick us up at six in the morning. We were glad we didn't need to hitchhike, as at the end of summer it can already get quite chilly at night. The sun was just rising when we drove off, with Anne and me sitting in the back and her face exuberating with excitement. She took my hand and whispered in my ear: "I'm so happy to go on this trip with you, Bernardo; I just know it's going to be wonderful." – "I am also glad to go with you, Anne. I'm leaving a whole hippie-commune and my cat. But when it's time to go, one must follow that inner voice." We arrived the same evening in Barcelona. It was too late to catch a plane, so we spent the night at a cheap pension in Barcelona. We were both very tired, but before dosing off to sleep, I could feel Anne's hand touching mine softly and it felt like waves of warm energy flowing through my whole body.

A Place Called Paradise

The next morning after some breakfast we took the train to the Barcelona airport and checked out the flights for that day to Tenerife. We found one that would leave at around eleven in the morning, which would bring us to Tenerife in time to catch the last boat for La Gomera at seven. Since the price sounded okay we happily bought our tickets. For both of us it was our first time on a plane and when we got lifted up into the sky, we felt like having left everything behind and going to land somewhere different and starting a new life.

Tenerife seemed quite dry, especially the south where we landed. There wasn't much lush greenery, but we had sort of gotten used to that already on Formentera. We did notice though the many cactuses and palm trees everywhere, which we both really enjoyed. We caught the bus to Los Cristianos and walked over to the port where we bought our tickets for the ferry. The boat-ride is only about an hour long and one can already see the island of La Gomera from Tenerife. There were quite a lot of hippies on the ferry, as well as some regular tourists and locals. It was a refreshing ride on the ship as we let the sea breeze blow through our hair. We had a much better view of Tenerife now and could see the majestic Mount Teide in the back, with its snowcap.

San Sebastian is the port city where we got off the ferry. We were told that it was too late to get to Valle Gran Rey; there was no more public transport there that night. So we were looking around for a cheap pension to spend the night. San Sebastian is the capital city of the island but looks much more like a village than a city. After finding a place to stay for the night, we went out to get some food and started talking to a hippie couple eating next to us. We were informed that there were basically two ways to get to Valle Gran Rey, one was with an old boat called 'Alcatraz', or else by bus over the mountains through the rainforest. One could also try to hitchhike but there are very few cars going there as the roads are bad. We'd heard the same thing before from Jaqueline.

"I really want to see the rainforest, that must be gorgeous," Anne suggested. So the next morning we caught the early bus. It was amazing how it started driving upward, curve after curve to finally about 1000 meters high. San Sebastian eventually looked like a small spot down by the ocean. The vegetation seemed to change after every few curves, from cactuses to palm trees to all kinds of bushes and trees. And we saw so many incredible rock-formations. What I found very interesting was that you could see palm trees growing on small ledges of some big rocks, it looked so amazing. We saw small houses spread out with goats and some vegetable gardens, where people basically live apart from the rest of the world. As we entered the rainforest, it was just amazing, as all trees were covered with moss from top to bottom and they seemed very lush and green.

We were told that it's the fog up here that keeps things humid in this forest that consists mainly of bay-trees. And sure enough, there were mystical clouds of fog sweeping over the rock formations and over the trees. At one turn you would see a mountain, but when trying to see it again after the next curve, it would already be covered in a cloud of fog. The fog was moving around fast which made this place look very much alive. At some places of the road, the rain-forest was so lush that the trees had intertwined with the trees on the other side of the road, causing the bus to drive through these green tunnels.

Going back down the mountain on the other side of La Gomera was quite a ride. Overlooking the whole Valle Gran Rey was a thrilling experience, as it was full of palm trees and greenery. Slowly the bus made its way back down to sea level, with some breathtaking curves. The road was only partially tarred, so it was a bit of a rocky ride and Anne was holding on to me more than once. "This valley is so totally beautiful", she said in astonishment. It was indeed, with small vil-lages on the side of the valley and very lush gardens in the middle where there seemed to be a riverbed, which was dry at the moment. "Yes, Anne, it does really look like paradise." Though I couldn't compare, as it's just an expression we use for a kind of place we wouldn't want to leave.

When we got out of the bus, we just followed the other hippies down to 'Casa Maria' where we had some lunch. 'Casa Maria' was sort of the main hip-pie-hangout and there were quite a lot of them sunbathing at the beach in front of it. We found out that many hippies would either find themselves a cheap pension or go sleep at 'Playa del Ingles', while some more adventurous ones would go to a remote stone-beach with natural caves that was called 'Bay of Pigs'. After discussing with Anne we agreed that we would both prefer sleeping under the stars to begin with, and so we made our way towards 'Playa del Ingles'. It turned out to be only about a fifteen minute walk.

The first thing we noticed were the beautiful sand dunes just before getting to the beach, with nice greenery on top of the sand and around the dunes. People had built small stone circles everywhere which were apparently for protection from too much sun or from the wind. The beach itself was very rocky with plots of black sand in between and tremendous waves splashing against the rocks. At the further end of this stony beach there were high cliffs, and right behind us, this 500 meter high mountain ascended. We needed to really raise our heads to look all the way to its top, it was standing so tall and with birds flying along the rocks. No road led any further, we felt like we had arrived at the end of the world.

"Any stone circle that is abandoned, you can just sort of claim for yourself and put your stuff in there". Some hippies mentioned the 'unwritten rules of the land' upon our arrival. So we got settled into this beautiful stone circle and were happy to put our backpacks and sleeping bags down between these rocks. Anne had this colourful Nepali drape which she put over it for some shade. We had noticed that almost everyone on the beach was nude and so we just did the same. It wasn't the first time I'd seen Anne nude but she was just stunningly beautiful. I had to actually sort look over to the mountain behind us as not to appear staring at her.

We made friends with a young German couple who were in the stone circle next to ours. Their names were Ben and Claire. Then we went to cool down a bit in the water, there were some places where the water had been splashing in over the rocks. It was so good to feel the salt-water again. From what we had heard, swimming out in the water there could be dangerous and some people who hadn't heeded the warnings had already paid with their lives. So whenever we wanted to go swimming in the future we would go to some other beaches that were much safer. It was a wild place, but the wildness held its own attraction.

As the sun was setting, a few hippies were gathering with a guitar and drums and we sat down with them to watch the sun set over the Atlantic Ocean. It had been a long trip getting here to what seemed like the edge of the world, far away from the hectic life up north, but it seemed worth it. Anne was leaning her head against my shoulder and we both watched the sun as it was trying to keep its last golden rays from falling, and to let their golden glow shine on for as long as possible. We were quite tired from the trip and went into our sleeping bags soon after.

"It was such an extraordinary day with that exciting bus ride, and then driving down this heavenly valley." Anne was holding and caressing my hand as we were looking up into the endless starry sky and listening to the waves crashing nearby. She moved closer and snuggled up to me. I felt very blessed having Anne with me and feeling her warm body through her sleeping bag. It was getting a bit chilly as the sun had disappeared a while ago, and the heat it had left on the rocks and the black sand had now cooled down. With this wonderful feeling of closeness to Anne I finally dosed off to sleep. I felt like all these gorgeous waves splashing all over me and carrying me away into eternal bliss.

I must have slept quite long because when I woke up, the sun was already up from behind the mountains, and shining on my face through the drape. Anne was sitting right outside our rock circle, enjoying the crashing of the waves. She had woken up about half an hour before I did; apparently we both had slept very long. I sat down beside her as we were looking at the sea for a while, and then decided that we would go look for some breakfast at 'Casa Maria'. We only took our documents and money with us, as we felt quite comfortable to leave the rest of our belongings at the beach. The crowd that was there didn't look like they would steal from us.

A few other people we had met the night before came along too, so we were quite a happy crowd arriving at 'Casa Maria' and ordering some 'cortado leche leche', which is a coffee specialty on the Canary Islands. Anne was hungrier than me and she ordered a 'tortilla', while I was happy with just a croissant. We all sat there watching the first hippies who were coming to set up their colourful towels to lie on. 'Playa Maria' was more public, and it wasn't a place where people would spend the night.

Generally it seemed the locals were very friendly towards the hippies. This could be partly due to their general open attitude towards life. Living very secluded from the rest of the world here, the people just lived from fishing and a bit of agriculture, so anyone coming to visit them seemed to be something that brought a bit of life into their seclusion. Later on I realized that many of the locals here were quite spiritually oriented, and that could be another reason that they sort of liked us hippies coming here. Some more regular tourists had started to find their way to Valle Gran Rey as well, which had brought in a bit of money, without any mass tourism.

Reset The World

Ben and Claire, the couple staying inside the stone circle next to ours, had come along for breakfast too. They were from Germany and had been together for about a year. After having done some studies, they had decided to leave everything behind for some time, in order to try out hippie life. They were a couple of years older than us and had already been here for a couple of months. Knowing the ropes, they were able to pass on some valuable information. They would rotate between staying at the beach overnight for some days, and staying sometimes in a pension. One could get a cheap apartment or stay in a pension for between 5 to 10 DM (German Mark), so they sometimes stayed in one of those in order to enjoy a bathroom, a kitchen, and a real bed.

At 'Playa del Ingles' these commodities were missing, but being together with so many hippies, combined with the proximity of the waves, made it a unique experience. As there was of course no fridge, one couldn't keep cold drinks, and this led to quite a bit of back and forth between the playa and the small 'tienda' (shop) in town. When going that direction we would ask other people if they needed anything from there; and when they were going that way they'd ask us the same. So we were all helping one another and there was a real sense of community among those of us who were staying at this beach. For right now, Anne and I both felt like we wanted to take in as much of this great atmosphere as we could, and we had slept quite comfortably on the soft sand.

We bought some water and things to make sandwiches with at 'Tienda Maria', and headed back for 'Playa del Ingles'. When we got there, we took our clothes off; that's what everyone else did too. You only had to put them back on when going to town, or when it was getting chilly. Ben and Claire came over, and we were all gathered there in front of our stone circles, on a large section of black sand that had accumulated between the rocks. The waves were splashing over the rocks in front, and you could see people walking along the beach, some in meditation, others looking for some nice rocks to take back home.

After eating some sandwiches, Anne offered to put some sun screen on my back, and it felt so good to feel her hands all over my back. Of course, then I did the same to her. Our skin was still quite white compared to some of the folks who had been here longer. I let my hands glide over the back of Anne's body, and since she didn't say 'stop', I just kept on. Ben and Claire were all over each other, it seemed like they really loved each other; it was nice to see that. I realized how much I missed having that sort of a romantic relationship with someone.

"Don't you all think it would be great if people lived more secluded and away from the world? That way they could spend more time taking in the beauty,

and would have less time for bad thoughts and stress."
Anne was formulating what had been going on in my
mind as well. "Yes, if somehow the world could stop
all this striving for material things, they would have
more time to listen to nature and to take in positive
vibes. Perhaps that might cause people to want to act
more lovingly and kindly towards each other."

"Well, Bernardo," Claire said, "the positive vibes
seem to get lost when people have to work long hours
at their jobs. Society should encourage people to go
back to their farms instead of luring them into coming
to work in factories to produce more electronic goods
we don't really need. We can't eat electronic goods.
The few farmers left in the world need to work their
ground many times over than what is good for mother
earth, in order to meet the demands of society. Humanity is digging its own grave!"

I could see Anne was really thinking about what
Claire had just said. "I'm starting to wonder if they'll
ever wake up. Maybe now with so many hippies questioning these things something might change."

Ben brought us somewhat back down to reality: "I
think it's an illusion to think that the world will
change, the people who are making money off producing all these material things won't allow it to happen.
They don't care about mother earth, they care for the
money." And Claire added: "And most people are
happy to have their TV to watch when they come
home from work, and depend on the security this materialistic world offers them. So, even the big masses in
this world don't really want to change anything." I
guess being a bit older than us they seemed to have
gathered a certain sense of reality which Anne and I

were still missing in our youthful enthusiasm. In some ways we still had maintained some hope that the world could be changed and somehow return back to a slower pace.

So Anne turned towards me and said: "Ben is right, Bernardo, we can't change the world, it's too evil. Why do you think the hippie-movement doesn't succeed? Because too many influential people don't want it to succeed. And who would want to listen to the hippies anyway? We can't change things peacefully and violence is no option for peaceful people like us. All we can do is go and live our own life-style in peace and love. That's our only hope!"

Claire was trying to cheer us up a bit. "You guys, wouldn't it be nice to have a reset-button and just undo all the damage mankind has ever done to every tree that was destroyed, every animal that was killed in selfishness, every blade of grass that had to give its life for a new road, every young person that was killed in some senseless war? I think this would be wonderful. Give me such a reset button and I will definitely use it!"

We all smiled about the reset-button idea. "Imagine having the world reset to the time before this big industrial revolution. I wonder how they kept their beer cold," Ben chuckled. "Talking about beer, I'll go get you all some cold drinks at 'Tienda Maria'." Claire was laughing: "See, we do appreciate some of the things the industrial revolution brought along, like a fridge. Not all were evil inventions, but mankind just doesn't find the brakes in their industrialization and destruction of mother earth and its resources. That's what's bad."

LONELY TRAVELLER

The sun started getting really hot at about two o'clock in the afternoon, though I was never really sure what time it was, I had stopped wearing a watch when we left Switzerland, and Anne didn't wear one either. She put up her Nepali drape over our stone circle, and we went under its shade, thinking about those things we had discussed. "Bernardo, if we can't change society, then we must do something to change ourselves. It's within our own hands to steer our lives in the direction we want it to go." "I agree, Anne, I think we've gotten a step closer today in seeing this more clearly."

Realities, Good Vibes
And Meditation

Anne was lying there with her eyes wide open, and in deep thought. "Bernardo, have you ever thought of what you're going to do long term?" - "Anne, I have told you before that I had visited a couple child-centers to see about job opportunities there." – "Yes, you did Bernardo, but you didn't tell me why you didn't take the job." I hated that question. It put my whole being and my future into question in front of my eyes. It was hard enough asking myself that question, let alone having someone else ask me about it. After a few thoughtful moments I said: "I do know these kids need the help of loving people, especially on that one farm where a handful of orphans were staying. The lady who was in charge there had a lot of love for the kids, I could see that. But I was thinking that I would just be there helping these kids to become part of a society that I myself didn't really want to be a part of. I think right now I am looking for some alternative ways to live, if they even exist. It might just turn out that there is no alternative to this society. Or that it might be too difficult to live an alternative life-style, I guess I'll find that out."

I could see certain sadness in Anne's eyes. "If I ever have children I would first want to find out what the goal in life is: what we are here for, and what moral code should I live by. Only then would I want to have children, once I know that. I'm really looking for some answers to these questions and hope things will become a bit clearer soon." It was time for a positive thought: "Well, Anne, I think what we discussed with Ben and Clare about facing reality has already really helped me. We need to take our lives into our hands and make the best of it. Just blaming society and what they're doing or not doing isn't going to bring us any further."

I could see her deep brown eyes looking at me and her lips broke into a big warm smile. Her face was so lovely and her long brown hair was like a gorgeous ornamental frame around her face. I knew I could fall in love with her, if she'd let me. But I already felt blessed as it was. It was so good to have found a soul mate to travel with. "Bernardo", she whispered, "I like you more and more every day."

Adding to the good mood we had gotten in was the fact that Ben had brought back some cold drinks. "You guys are really sweet, we're happy we met you", Anne told them. "The pleasure is ours", Ben said while Claire smiled and nodded her head.

It was getting really hot now and we all lay down some more in the shade. Anne kept staring into my eyes and I felt too much like kissing her when she looked at me like that, so I just closed my eyes and must have dosed off to sleep. I had probably slept for a couple of hours, when I was woken up by the sound of drums nearby. The sun was still up, but it seemed like it was going to take a while until sunset. My stomach sent some signals, and I went to look for Anne, to find out about dinner. She was sitting at the shore with Ben and Claire, and they had already been discussing about the four of us going for dinner together; we could get 'paella'. That idea definitely got me awake again, and the four of us started walking towards 'Casa Maria'.

'Casa Maria', I was told, was pretty much the first restaurant where hippies came to eat at. There was another one next to it on the beach called 'Yaya' and there were some more restaurants in 'Vueltas', which was situated near the port, and where one could get fresh fish. 'Vueltas' was about a half an hour walk away from our camp, but today we didn't feel like walking so far, so we settled for 'Yaya'. The paella was delicious and we ordered a large jar of chilled 'sangria' with it. The nice thing about 'sangria' is that it's very refreshing with ice and fruit juice in it. It doesn't only leave you with a buzz from the alcohol, but also kind of quenches your thirst. You'll see us drink this quite often as the story goes on.

The sun had started to set by now, and we could hear the sound of drums and guitars coming in from the beach in front of 'Casa Maria'. The few tables were full, and many people were standing around just having a drink and watching the sunset while listening to the hippie music. We weren't planning on eating out every day, but now that we had just arrived we still had quite some money, and we were really hungry. The food was incredibly tasty, the 'sangria' was strong, and the sunset awesome, the drums and guitars fascinating, and the atmosphere at the table was happy and cheerful. We got to know lots of things about Ben and Claire.

They had hitchhiked from Frankfurt, Germany, all the way down along the Spanish coast to Gibraltar, from where they had been able to get on a freighter very cheaply to cross over to Las Palmas on Gran Canaria. They had continued on over here on a couple boats. Ben had finished his master degree, and was thinking of going to study further to get his doctorate. Claire had already done one year of university studies, but took leave, as she didn't really know which direction she should go with her studies. Both of them were fascinated by the hippie life-style. They had been together for nearly a year now and just wanted to get away from their regular situation for a while, in order to get their thoughts and lives sorted out.

"It must be quite reassuring to know what you want to do", I said to Ben. "Hmm…," he replied. "It's sort of laid out before me to go in that direction, but I don't like society. If I do continue to study medicine, I want to go help some poor people later on." – "That's what I would like to do as well, Ben, to help people in some way; that seems to be the only thing that's worth living for. I'm not going to work for the economy, even though that's what I've learned."

The girls had gotten into a conversation of their own, and Ben said: "I think the important thing is to not let oneself be driven by the desire for career and money, but to look for ways to contribute something positive to this world. Yet, I think you're right. It has to come from within and not from something others want or expect of you." Claire must have overheard something, because she looked at me as if she had been reading my thoughts, and said: "Bernardo, don't compare your journey with Ben's. He seems to already have an idea of what to do and where to go with his life, and at the moment, you don't. I myself don't know either, but I think each one of us has their own journey, their own destiny, and each one of us must try to find it at our own pace and time. It's not some sort of a competition, it's your life." I smiled: "I really like you for saying that...wise lady."

I liked both of them, they were sweet and sincere, and I felt very comfortable around them. They seemed to emit a certain amount of maturity, and I was looking forward to getting to know them better. Claire seemed a bit like she could be Anne's older sister, and she had that same air of freedom and wildness, yet at the same time with both feet on the ground. It's a combination I really liked and admired in women. Claire had long blonde hair and blue eyes, and she wore this beautiful silky lilac colored dress, which must have come from the East, and a necklace made of seashells. When she'd look at you with her blue eyes, it was like you could see and hear the waves of the ocean and get lost. Ben had brownish curly long hair, similar to the main singer in the movie 'Hair', and a three-month long beard, as he probably hadn't shaved since he had left on this trip. He wore a brown leather vest, and the color of his skin was so brown by now that it almost matched the color of his vest. He wore this beautiful leather bracelet on his arm with blue and red gems, as well as bits of lava rock.

LONELY TRAVELLER

It was nearly dark by the time we got back to 'Playa del Ingles', but we could still see the last shimmer of golden light across the sky where the sun had disappeared on the horizon. It looked like quite a lot more people had arrived today, and some were propped up on their backpacks and just taking a rest from the long trip. We sat a while longer with Ben and Claire in front of our stone enclosures, watching and listening to the waves. "There is this one hippie who brings coffee to the beach in the morning", Ben said. "That way you can get a coffee before having to go get it in town; you just need to get up a bit earlier tomorrow." – "I think I will. I feel rested up, and I am the kind of person that tends to get up quite early," I replied. Claire added: "We bought some fresh buns at 'Tienda Maria' today, so we can have some breakfast together." That sounded great. Ben and Claire went over to their stone circle, and we could hear them giggling and kissing.

Anne seemed to get a bit dreamy when she heard them. "It's nice when people are so in love. I thought I was in love with Pierre too, but I found out it was more infatuation than love." She had gone back to the house one day as she had forgotten a painting that a customer wanted, and there she had found Pierre in bed with another girl whom she had never seen before. Anne hadn't told me the details before. "It didn't hurt so much in an emotional sense, Bernardo. I wasn't that much in love or attached to him in that way, but it hurt that it was just going on without me knowing anything, and so I felt I didn't want to stay there any longer. I haven't been with anyone romantically or sexually since then. I've started to appreciate true friends a lot more, and I began to see friendship as something far more important. During my time in Switzerland, I had gotten a lot closer to my friend Jaqueline, the one who had told me about La Gomera. She helped me a lot in sorting out my mind about my broken relationship with Pierre."

As I went to lie down for the second night, Anne was staying up a bit longer. I really liked Anne, not just as a friend. I didn't really know how she felt about me, but I started having real feelings for her. She was a beautiful girl and there was a lot that attracted me about her looks. But her personality was what held the biggest attraction for me. I liked the way she thought about things so deeply and her openness in formulating her thoughts. I liked the way she was so bubbly and alive and the way she would get so enthusiastic and passionate about things she loved.

Anne came to lie down too, and after a couple of minutes, I could feel her hand touching mine and it felt so comforting and peaceful. "Sometimes I feel like these stars are not just lights in the sky, but that they're trying to communicate with us. The stillness of the night can be so loud," she whispered. She really connected at night, while I was more the sort of person who connected in the early hours of the day.

I woke up early the next day. People around me in the other shelters and around the sand dunes were still sleeping, and there was no one up yet. It was a wonderful feeling to be living among all these lovely people, and it made me feel so much at home. It was a similar feeling to what I had experienced at Vondelpark in Amsterdam, but this time totally out in nature. I enjoyed getting up before everyone else did, there was something magical about this. You can reflect on your thoughts totally undisturbed while others are still asleep. You can hear the sounds of nature which the tumult of the day shuts out. Only the first roosters on nearby farms made themselves to be heard, announcing a new day with such a joyous sound.

At the far end of the beach I noticed a guy strolling around, and letting the waves touch his feet. The sun hadn't come up over the steep cliffs behind us yet, so it was still a bit chilly. I took my jacket and went along the beach, looking for pretty stones which the waves had washed ashore. Bill was his name; he was Canadian. He had been here for a year. "The first hippies that had come here were Americans and Canadians. Many would move on to India and Nepal later. Later on, more and more European hippies started coming down here," he said. "My brother had lived here for a few months, and then he moved on to Amsterdam. From there he went on to India and Nepal. It must have been up in Amsterdam where word had spread about La Gomera". Amsterdam seemed to be indeed one of the main hippie communication centers in those days.

Bill told me that he had started to make his own jewelry from lava rocks and nice stones that he had found here. He was making enough that way to get by. He had lived with a Spanish girl up on a 'finca' (piece of land with garden) and they had grown their own vegetables. Apparently, a few days ago they broke up, so he came back to the beach. "I'm glad she hadn't gotten pregnant, or it would have been a lot more difficult to leave," he added. Didn't really know what to think about that as I wasn't about to get anyone pregnant.

And if it were to happen, this would be considered a serious matter and bring problems my way which I didn't even want to think about at this point. Well, it wasn't a problem for now as I had been careful not to cause any 'accidents'. And I could hardly remember the last time I had sex. I started wondering about that too.

Bill was a very handsome guy, his skin tanned by the eternal sun here on the island, and he wore a cool jeans vest which someone must have had embroidered for him in a painstakingly beautiful work of oriental flowers. 'Wait until Anne sees this guy', I thought to myself. He certainly seemed to be a lot flashier than me, I thought. Perhaps I felt a bit insecure around people who knew what they were doing, or who had certain talents or looks which I didn't. That may have added to the dilemma I had with my self-esteem in those days. But thankfully I had started to realize that such comparing didn't really bring me anywhere and that it was my own spiritual connection that would give me something to hold on to.

I wanted to know more about the selling of jewelry, and how he did it. "I go sell them at 'Baby Beach' and in 'Vueltas', or sometimes in front of 'Casa Maria'. There are not just hippies coming here now, main tourism has found its way down here as well. The tourists bring a bit more money than the hippies, and want to bring home some hand-made souvenirs. My ex-girlfriend, who I have just broken up with, got me into this. We used to do all the jewelry at our 'finca' and then sell it to the tourists, she still does it. We also sell some to the shops, or at the hippie market."

I was glad I had started talking to this guy. "My friend Anne is very good at making stuff with her hands, and she has lots of experience in sales." – "Just go up to 'El Guro', it's the next village up the hill, and ask for 'Maria la joyera' (Maria the jeweler), everyone knows her." I was glad for this info, as Anne would probably be thrilled to get more info and access to people that were already doing it.

When I got back, Anne was getting up, and I had exciting news for her. "Wow, Bernardo! That would be a dream." At this moment, I saw the guy coming with two large thermos bottles and plastic cups hanging on him, and thought this might be the coffee-hippie that Ben had mentioned. "Ben, are you awake? I think the coffee-brother is here." So Ben and I went to organize some coffee for the four of us, and then we all enjoyed our little breakfast on the heap of black sand in front of our stone circles. We told them what I had just found out from Bill, and Claire said: "Anything that gets one so excited in the morning is always good news. Anyway, Ben and I decided that since we're running out of money soon, we'll return to Germany before we're broke. We aren't really into producing anything that could bring us some money here. We had been talking half the night, and a lot of things have become a lot clearer to us regarding our future. It must be the waves and the stars." We were really happy for them, but a bit sad to hear they'll be leaving. "But we'll stay a bit longer, we like you guys a lot, and want to show you some of the places we got to know," Ben said. "If you want, we'd like to walk with you to 'Vueltas' today. On the way there we could stop at 'Charco Del Conde', where there is a nice little beach called the 'Baby

Beach', probably because it's so small. But the nicest beach is at the port, it's called 'Playa de Vueltas'. Let's go before the sun gets too hot, it's a bit of a walk." That sounded like an exciting excursion.

So we walked through 'La Playa', passing by 'Casa Maria' where we had dinner the night before, and along the seaside through 'La Puntilla'. The waves weren't high today, and there was a very peaceful atmosphere. The less noise the waves made, the more one could hear the birds. We passed by lots of banana plantations, and there were all kinds of other things growing in between. "Tio Pepe sells fresh fruits and veggies, he's not open yet, but we can pick up some on the way back," Claire mentioned. "Fresh mangos, papayas, avocados, bananas and tomatoes, all sun-ripened."

The waves at 'Playa del Ingles' were just too high to go in all the way, so we had only splashed ourselves a little bit without really going into the sea. But we were all the happier to go in at 'Baby Beach', which was a small lake with large rocks blocking the sea. The waves were splashing fresh sea-water into it continuously. It was very refreshing and we were glad that we had brought our bathing suits, because the tourists there were all 'properly' dressed as this one wasn't a nudist beach.

Arriving at 'Vueltas', we noticed a few restaurants and bars as well as a few hippie shops. The small streets were very fascinating, it looked like this was the old part of town. 'Playa de Vueltas' was so beautiful with deep blue sea water and without the waves coming in. The shore was protected from the waves by the walls of the harbor, so one could do some nice swimming there. We could see all kinds of fish swimming around and we even noticed a beautiful 'Medusa' floating along. They can really sting, but we weren't about to get that close to it. If one keeps their distance from them, they are beautiful to look at and they won't swim up to you, at least not the kind we saw, they just float on the sea.

A few wooden fishing boats in all kinds of colors were anchored in the bay, but there was still plenty of space to swim. The whole scene had one thing in common with 'Playa del Ingles': The high cliffs and mountains that were ascending right up from the sea behind the beach. There was a small road that had been carved at the bottom of the cliff, and Ben explained to me that it reached over to a beautiful 'finca'. "And right behind it you could climb over this huge pile of rocks in order to get to the 'Bay of Pigs', with some natural caves where some hippies are staying." That must be fascinating, I thought.

"Have you been there, Ben?" I asked. "Yes, Claire and I went there one day. We had actually taken all of our stuff with us, as we thought we may stay there for some time. We only ended up staying one night, as it's a bit far from everything. If you need a bottle of drinking water, or anything, you have to go all the way back to 'Vueltas' each time, climbing over rocks and walking right on the bottom of this steep cliff where rocks could fall at any time." I was at least hoping to get to see those caves in the future and see who lives there. "Bernardo, the people who live there are probably of the kind that like to be a bit secluded. You are far too social for that," Anne mentioned. "Well, maybe it would do me good to go into some seclusion again," I replied.

The times I had gone into seclusion had really helped me in finding a spiritual connection, and it had done me a lot of good each time. Lately I'd found my times of quietness mainly in the morning, by getting up early and going on a stroll and then sitting down somewhere to meditate and pray. I am indeed the kind of person who needs people around and I can't be away from people for too long.— "How about you, Anne?" Claire asked. "Well, in that sense I'm a bit like Bernardo. I can't be alone for too long either. But I do take time to meditate and pray, often in the evening before going to sleep." I realized she might have stayed up doing that the night before, when she didn't come to sleep right away.

The Essence Of Life

We had some boccadillos (Spanish sand-wiches) at 'El Puerto', which was right next to the harbor. "Why do you think the world has gotten so strange?" I asked Claire. I was try-ing to get more information from the unseen reservoir of wisdom she seemed to have. "Well, Bernardo, I per-sonally think the world has always been a bit strange ever since it started being populated by mankind. Any history book shows that the strong was always trying to control the weak. And the industrial revolution made people probably even greedier. It just advanced to another level, and I suppose it made people more stressed, instead of providing them with the happiness they had expected." That was interesting.

"So you're sort of talking about two different things here. On one hand you're saying that some peo-ple have always been greedy and that's why wars and abuse have been around ever since humanity came into existence. And on the other hand you're saying that the process sort of got accelerated by the indus-trial revolution?" Claire smiled: "You got it, Bernardo."

Now it was Ben's turn: "But the industrial revolution also sped up the process of destruction of mother earth. Many people weren't happy staying on farms, as they were lured into getting those new gadgets that the industrial revolution offered. Many left farming for what seemed like more lucrative factory jobs in the big cities. The industrial factories were and are detrimental to the well-being of mother earth, to its nature and animals. George Orwell might have been quite accurate in his visions about the future in his book called '1984'. The world seems to be heading that way."

I thought about that for a moment. "Well, hopefully it will take a little longer to get that bad; we may not see that day." Anne looked at me, and I could see something was bothering her about what I had said. "Bernardo, you may not live to see the world getting that bad, but your children will, in case you might have any." She was right. I couldn't just think about my life only, just hoping to live my life in a world that stayed halfway intact. What kind of world will we be leaving behind for future generations? "Maybe that's why I don't want to have any children, Anne. But you're right, it's wrong to only think about our own life. I for sure don't want to partake in this race for materialism that is wasting the world's resources."

Anne continued with a somewhat cynical smile: "You say you don't want to partake in this race, Bernardo. The world and society call people who don't agree with the way things are being done in this world 'antisocial'. But I think that the opposite is the case: People who feel concerned about their fellowman and mother earth often behave a lot more responsibly and lovingly towards other people and towards nature, its resources and the animals."

It was an extensive discussion, like so many of our discussions which would often continue way into the night. Some people may chuckle and say: "But you guys didn't find any answers! " This may be partially true. But at least we were thinking. At least we didn't just close our eyes to a system that is going the wrong direction. At least we dreamed of a better world and tried to live it in our own way. As a matter of fact I'd like to add here that hippies were usually very friendly and kind, sharing their food or a bed for the night whenever needed. They were very tolerant and non-judgmental, which made one feel loved and accepted

We went on our way back to 'Playa del Ingles', and each of us seemed a bit quiet. Anne was holding my arm and looking out to the sea, which was quite calm today. "Even though we can't really change the course this world takes, we can still live the principles we believe in as much as possible. Because a life not being spent in loving others and mother earth is a life wasted. A life spent only in gaining materialism is a life wasted as well, and a life spent in only focusing on things seen without seeking the energy behind is also a life wasted."

"I agree on that, Anne. The essence of life is love. I think freedom is important too. It's difficult to love when being attached or chained to so many material things, because they take so much of our attention away from love. And I also think it's difficult for people who are exploited by others to feel free to love, as such unkind treatment often provokes hate."

SERENO SKY

The sun had gotten really hot by now, and many people had apparently already started 'siesta', as the shops were closed and the streets empty. Except for the beach at 'Playa Maria', where some sun-hungry tourists seemed to be grilling themselves in hope of going back home with a tan.

As were laying down for a 'siesta', Anne caressed my hair and said in a gentle tone: "I just want to have a happy life with as few chains as possible. Responsibility is enough of a chain, one that we bear with courage and love for those we are responsible for. I don't want to take on all those other chains that drag us down and make life heavy."

When I woke up, the sun was already quite low and it was time for the sunset gathering. Anne was sitting there and talking intensely with Claire. "Oh, Bernardo, that walk had knocked you out." Both girls were sitting there smiling at me. "It wasn't just the walk; it was our interesting conversation over lunchtime as well." It was so nice to see the two girls talking together. I liked both of them, but I realized that my love for Anne was growing day by day, and I found myself looking forward to her touching my hand again before going to sleep.

Ben had gone to town and brought back some nice Spanish red wine. I saw a set of congas on the sand with this one brother who was busy rolling a joint, and he let me use it to drum along. It was nice to follow the rhythm, adding my own little taps. What I always found so nice about this type of jamming session was in there being totally nothing commercial about it: Just an expression of the feelings and vibrations of the moment.

"That was an exciting day again, Bernardo, wasn't it?" Anne said later on as she put her hand on mine before going to sleep, and I squeezed it. I wanted her to know that I really enjoyed her soft touches. "It was great and there were a lot of interesting thoughts to digest from these discussions. It was so sweet of Ben and Claire to take us around. I'm just so happy we came down here, it's a spiritual trip every day". - "Yes Bernardo, many of the things that come up are helping me to see where I want to go in life and what kind of person I want to be. Slowly but surely I am able to see my ideology more clearly, finding the morals and ethics I want to live by." I could see in her eyes that this day had brought new hope to her. "Anne, I wanted to tell you that I really like it when you touch my hand." She smiled: "I was really hoping you would, Bernardo."

The next morning Bill was there again, strolling around looking for rocks, and as soon as Anne woke up I introduced her to him. She was very excited, as she was hoping he'd have more information on "Maria la joyera'. "I will take you there today. I know she's home," Bill said. I could see Anne's eyes lit up, sort of like a little girl who had just been told by her daddy that he would take her to a fairground. I knew it meant a lot to her. She certainly had the talent, and was probably missing getting her hands on stuff and being creative. The things I'd seen her produce before we had left on this trip were absolutely gorgeous.

I decided to stay back, as I wanted to take a quiet day to myself, to find some time for meditation. So, after getting our morning coffee from our 'hippie-café', Anne and Bill left. Anne said she didn't know when she was going to be back, but the walk up to 'El Guro' would take about forty-five minutes, and then she was going to try to spend as much time as possible finding out about the possibility of making her own jewelry. Ben had decided to go up on top of the mountain behind us, the 'Mirador de la Américas'. In order to get up there he would take some transportation up the valley and then it would be almost a straight walk to get there. Claire seemed a bit worried, but said: "As long as you don't climb up these steep cliffs behind us in order to get up there I will be all right."

As for me it was time to shut down my brain a bit, as it had taken in much input over the last days. I strolled towards the end of the beach, where there were only cliffs and one couldn't go any further, and sat on a rock. As I was closing my eyes, I could only hear the crashing of the waves. I felt this warmth again which I had experienced on 'Mont Soleil'. I realized that all I had to do was just stop and want to connect, and there it was again; that beautiful warm feeling that brought so much peace.

My next thought was that I could really use some guidance right now, and perhaps I could ask some questions. I wanted to know about Anne, and what part she played in my life. Sure enough, I did hear that inner voice again, or perhaps it was an outer voice, but that didn't matter much. What mattered is what I felt or heard so strongly: "Anne is a good person; she only means well. Be good to her." It couldn't have been any clearer. I felt very thankful for this 'info', and wanted to know about some other things as well.

One thing that was often bothering me at that time was the fact that I just had no idea where I was going in my life. I wanted to do something useful. I did want to make some money too so as not to become a burden on others. I would say at this point that the majority of hippies were never parasites and they did whatever necessary to make their own money. It was never my idea to live off the money of other hard-working people.

Again the voice answered: "It is her time now, your time will come." It was amazing to me how I could ask questions I had and then receive such specific and clear answers. I felt I was really getting somewhere spiritually, and it was an exciting new trip for me. For the first time I felt I didn't need to worry so much about my life, but that I could just connect and get help and guidance.

When Love Hurts

Later on I walked to town with Claire to get a something to eat. We were talking about Ben and his desire for adventure, and that she was a bit worried. "I heard that the road that goes up there from behind the mountain is quite safe, he'll be okay", I told her to help calm her down. I mentioned that I was worried a bit about Anne too. "I guess I'm just a bit jealous." – "I know what that feels like, Bernardo. We had some similar situations in our relationship at the beginning," Claire said. "It was beautiful but also a bit tough at the same time, until our love settled a bit, and now we both feel quite secure with each other." "But", she added, "Anne wants only the best for you." Well, now I'd heard almost the same thing from two different sources.

After getting back, I went to lie down a bit as the hot sun had gotten me tired. Claire stayed up sunbathing, and reading a book. It was getting close to sunset when I got up and was looking around for Anne. I noticed that she still hadn't come back and I started getting a bit worried, and Bill being so extremely handsome added to my worries. I was listening to the waves; at the way they first make this huge roar upon impact, and then softly roll out on the shore with a gentle and peaceful tone. But in my head the jealousy kept roaring, and it didn't roll out gently. I hadn't experienced such a thing, ever. Perhaps I hadn't really been in love, which meant that now I probably was.

I asked Ben and Claire if they had seen her, but they hadn't. Ben had just gotten back from the mountain. "You just hitch-hike the road up the valley, and then it's almost a straight walk to the mountain, with no steep uphill climbing. One just needs to be sure not to get too close to the cliff. I was almost sure I could see you guys down here as I noticed our stone circles." I tried to stay calm but was worried about Anne; less now about her and Bill starting something, but more just about her safety and why she was so late.

So I went to the circle in the sand where people would meet to play music. I thought it might distract me a little. 'Take in some smoke and forget about it', I thought to myself. I don't know if that helped me, but what did help me was that Claire came and sat beside me. "Ben's too tired to stay up. Bernardo, perhaps it might be better for you not to smoke too much grass at the moment, since you are worrying about Anne. You know how marihuana enhances your present mood." I knew that well enough and she was right. So I tried to stay calm and listen to that voice again, and I could hear a faint "she's all right" inside of me.

I was glad to have Claire beside me. I had gotten to like her, and even just her presence made me feel a touch more at ease. She put her arm on my shoulder and said: "You seem to like her a lot, Bernardo". I nodded. "Well, from all I've seen she likes you a lot too.

She told me the other night that travelling with you has been the most beautiful trip of her life so far, and she feels very comfortable around you. She told me she was sort of scared to give her heart to someone again as last time she had gotten hurt." The thundering waves started mellowing out a bit in my head after Claire had said that. "Thank you for mentioning that, it really helps. I don't know what's going to happen with us, Claire, but I just realized today that I love her a lot more than I first thought. I think I really fell in love with her. I miss her when she's not around."

It was after about an hour of sitting there and the sun having set in the meantime, that I saw Anne and Bill walking towards us. "Bernardo, this was such an exciting day!" she exclaimed happily as she hugged me and sat down with us. Bill sat down a while too, but left shortly after. "That's nice", I said, "but I started getting a bit worried, it got a bit late." Anne started telling us everything that had happened that day, and how she was able to meet Maria and see her workshop with all the different materials she uses to produce things with." She looked so happy and thrilled. "She also does beautiful 'crochet' stuff. I'd love to make some of those as well. You wouldn't believe all the different things she makes. There is hardly anything growing on this island that she doesn't use or recycle for some kind of product. She showed me those mysterious lamp shades cut out of the bark of old cactuses that have died; you would love them." She was just sparkling with excitement and I could see that this day had done her lot of good.

"Bill had invited me to go eat afterwards, that's why it got a bit late. I will go to Maria again the day after tomorrow; she will let me use some of her material. She also does yoga and has bi-weekly gatherings. I really want to go and attend those as well. It was such an exciting day for me. And what did you do today, Bernardo?" Well, my day hadn't been so spectacular, or maybe it had been, but I didn't know how to put it into a few words. So I just told her that I had spent part of the day meditating and that I had gone on a walk with Claire.

I guess she could feel that I wasn't in such a good mood tonight, but I guess no one can always be in a good mood. Later on, as we lay down in our sleeping bags, she cuddled up next to me. "I'm sorry it got a bit late, Bernardo. Bill wanted to talk; he is a sad man at the moment, because he still loves her very much. One of Maria's friends had seen him one evening making out with a girl in the dunes and told her about it. Now she doesn't want him back even though he admits it was a mistake, but it's hard on him. I guess he has some growing up to do and it's painful. He opened up to me, and even though I didn't really know what to say, I think it helped him that I was listening to him."

I was about to tell her about the jealousy I had been feeling, but in reality she hadn't done anything wrong, and I heard that still small voice again telling me, or reminding me, of what I'd heard this morning: "Be good to her". So I made peace with my jealousy monster, or looked at it straight in the eye, whatever. I put my arm under her head for the first time and she snuggled up to me. "I told Bill about my own experience of being hurt by Pierre and that it doesn't feel nice to get hurt. I really don't want to get hurt again, that's why I've been keeping to myself as far as romantic feelings go." That does make sense, I thought. "I was so happy to come back to you tonight, Bernardo. I hope you had a good day." - "I did, Anne, I really did." We were looking at the stars above for a few more minutes, and just before dosing off to sleep I noticed she had put one of her arms around me. I felt her body close to mine and thought to myself. "I really love that girl, I really do."

Beautiful Mother Earth

The next day we had nothing planned, except going to eat somewhere later in the day with Ben and Claire. We couldn't just live off of sandwiches. "Why don't we go to the port at 'Vueltas' and ask one of the fishermen if we could rent his boat for a while. At this hour they're not out at sea, and it is calm today; we could glide along the coast", Ben suggested. This man had adventure in his blood, it sounded great! So off we went, stopping by one of the local bars to get some 'cortado leche leche' and a Spanish tortilla.

When we arrived at 'Playa de Vueltas', we met a Spanish guy strolling along the beach, looking for shells, and we greeted him and started a conversation. Manolo and his girlfriend Monique had a boat, and they had come all the way from Alicante, Spain. Having left the mainland about a year ago and having stopped at various places on the way, they were now taking tourists out to sea, living off the money they got for it. We agreed on a good price and they were very happy to take us out, informing us that 'sangria' would be included.

Their boat was quite large; it had a sail, but was also fitted with quite a strong motor. They showed us around their boat, which consisted of a bedroom, a small kitchen and a toilet below deck. "We try to use the sail most of the time, but we do need the motor for certain situations. Today the sea is very quiet, so we have a good chance at seeing some dolphins," Manolo informed us. "But we can't promise anything, as often we don't see any, and then people are disappointed."

Anne wanted to know if they don't just flee when they notice a boat approaching. Manolo explained that they seem to be very playful creatures, and would often swim along the boat as if competing in a race. It must be nice to be so involved with these beautiful creatures and we were all hoping to see some. Manolo headed out to sea, as apparently the dolphins wouldn't come close to shore where the water wasn't so deep. He was scanning with his binoculars, and we hadn't been out long, when he spotted something. He passed the binoculars around, and sure enough, there were two or three of them just a couple hundred meters ahead of us.

Manolo slowed down the motor, mainly because of the noise, and we were now gliding pretty quietly towards them. As we got closer, he turned it off. Now we could see them as they came swimming around the boat, probably checking us out. There were three of them, and they didn't seem to be bothered by our presence. They didn't do any of their beautiful jumps though, but we were just watching like in a dream. "They're just so beautiful and peaceful", Anne said. Manolo started the motor again and we were driving off. They accompanied us for a while and were doing small jumps, then disappeared, only to jump up somewhere else again. It was fascinating and we were just in total awe. I looked over to Anne and I could see how touched she was by all this. When the dolphins totally disappeared, Manolo drove us towards the cliffs on the coast. We were all just stunned by what we'd seen. Manolo and Monique had seen the dolphins and also some whales there quite frequently, but for the rest of us it was the first time.

Ahead of us, we saw beautiful rock formations in various colors; it looked like nature had piled up different layers of stone on top of each other. At the bottom, where the waves were splashing ashore, we noticed various sized caves which the waves had washed out over time, some smaller and other larger ones. The wave would approach and when it hit one of those caves, it crashed into intensive sparkling white foam with innumerable drops of water exploding into the air. The shows that nature performs make this world such an incredibly beautiful place.

We were now heading back to Valle del Rey, gliding along very close to the coastline along the cliffs and then into this bay with a stone beach. This whole opening was the end of a canyon with a dry riverbed coming down. We noticed some abandoned houses, gardens, as well as some palm trees. "There was a salt flat here before," Manolo explained. "The water used to reach to the beach front, carrying fresh saltwater into those fields over there, where it would then dry out, leaving only the salt. It was then collected and brought to be used in an old abandoned fish-factory that we'll see later." No road was coming down this valley, so they must have transported the salt by ship. He anchored the boat out in the bay, and we all enjoyed some nice skinny dipping in the deep blue waters, drying ourselves on deck afterward. We were listening to some good music from a battery-operated player while drinking dark crimson 'sangria'. It was one of those moments one would like to just be able to push some kind of a 'pause' button, and let time stand still

"As you can see, there is no road coming down this valley. The people who worked here had to come by boat, maybe some lived here all the time and food and water was brought to them. We're now approaching the next canyon and there you will see the fish-factory." Manolo seemed to be the perfect guide, and with this boat, he had fulfilled his dreams. His father had been a fisherman, and taken him out to sea already in his childhood. When his father prematurely died in a storm, Manolo didn't want to take over the family business. "Too much hippie blood", he said with a big smile. So his mom sold some of the fishing boats in order to help him get his dream boat. "My mother 'es un angel' (my mother's an angel) and I call her almost every day from the payphone at Valle del Rey, as she really cares and worries." That reminded me that it would be good for Anne and me to call home that night, letting our parents know that we're okay. I guess people here seemed to have a different mentality, and stronger ties to their parents then some of us from up north did.

The fishery seemed totally abandoned. "They used to put sardines and tuna into cans and then ship them to the mainland Spain. People don't eat canned fish here, why should they," our captain explained, as we continued back towards the port of Valle del Rey.

"I heard that at one point the owners of this factory didn't want to pay higher wages, so the workers went on strike and the factory never opened up again." I guess the poor don't like to be underpaid, I thought. But instead of paying more, some entrepreneurs just moved their business elsewhere where it comes cheaper for them. There is this never ending struggle between the rich and the poor.

"It looks like we'll pass right by the hippie-caves at the 'Bay of Pigs'", I said with some excitement as I had really wanted to see that place. We couldn't get too close because of the waves, but some hippies were coming out and waving at us. They had also built some stone walls similar to the ones at the beach we had, probably for protection from the waves. During high tide the waves would get quite close. "Once a storm washed out everything, but no one was there, as the hippies had left to safety," Manolo explained. "It's not such a safe place to live, sometimes rocks fall down from the cliffs above, and it's also a bit complicated to bring water and food here." We could see colorful paintings on the walls, and some people were playing the drums and flute. "People here are very cool, but the place is a bit uncomfortable for staying longer". Anne had been quiet up until now, but I guess she was hoping that I didn't get any ideas of moving out here. She had been quite brave in sleeping out on the sandy beach, but any more 'hardships' might be a bit too uncomfortable for her, which I understood and respected.

"Bernardo, I think I like it where we are now. But it's nice that some hippies are so adventurous to live out here in those caves. I'd be a bit scared," she said. "It's no issue, Anne. I think they have it quite difficult to bring food and water out here. I do enjoy the Spanish hippie bringing us a coffee in the morning, and most of all I really love sleeping on the soft sand next to you." You should have seen her eyes and the smile she returned.

After getting back to the port, we thanked Manolo and Monique profusely for the wonderful time. They were such precious people, and they had found great pleasure in taking us around and catering to our needs. Being able to see the dolphins that day had been the icing on the cake and Anne was certainly on cloud seven. As we parted after warm hugs, they both waved us goodbye, and upon our leaving, Monique said with her French charm: "We're always here at the port at night, or at the restaurant 'el Puerto' and at 'Casa Maria', bonne journée à vous tous!" I just loved French, what a happy and friendly language.

Since we were hungry by now, we stopped at one of the restaurants in 'Vueltas'. This time each of us ordered something different; I had some pasta with fresh tuna accompanied by a beer. Anne looked so happy. "It was great, Anne, wasn't it?" She didn't say anything; she was caught in a dream.

It was Claire who said: "I think going to see the wild animals the way we did today seems okay if doing it carefully and with great respect, as Manolo did when turning off the motor. I just don't like those zoos. They had been built along with the industrial revolution when droves of people were moving to cities. They needed some attractions and the zoos happened to be one of them. They are like prison for those poor animals!" Claire had such a good heart. "You're right, Claire, and I wouldn't want to be put in a zoo for people to come stare at me either." Of course, people would always bring up the argument that animals in zoos don't know that they used to be free. But I think that animals often know more than us humans do!

We called our parents on the way back. They were happy to hear from us and that we were doing well. We shared some of the highlights, things that they would probably enjoy too, such as seeing the dolphins. They did ask if we're going to have a phone soon and we indicated that we'll be working on it. We did a bit of shopping on the way back and then headed for our camp. The sun was hot and it was time for 'siesta'. We thanked Ben and Claire for having taken us along on this excursion.

As we got back and lay down in our camp, Anne said: "I really enjoyed this, Bernardo. This has been one of the most beautiful days of my life. I would really like to go sit by the sea with you later on if you want." I didn't need to reply, she could just see the answer in my eyes.

After 'siesta' I wrote down a few highlights from the morning into my booklet, while Anne was reading 'Les Misérables' by Victor Hugo. "It had been mandatory reading at school", she said, "but now that it's not mandatory, I really want to read it again. It's such a beautiful story about love and forgiveness". I wasn't into any books since starting off on this trip; I had too many other impressions to digest at the moment. I had read so much before: Hermann Hesse, John Steinbeck, Sigmund Freud, Friedrich Nietzsche, Dom Helder Camaro, Jerry Rubin, the New Testament, Buddha, the Bhagavad Gita and many more, and they had all added things that had prepared me for my inner search. But at this point I felt it was time to make my own experiences and sort out my own thoughts, and so I hadn't been reading anything since we left.

I went over to a group of hippies who had arrived that morning, and this is where I met Peter and Sue. I could tell right away that they both came from Switzerland, as we Swiss-Germans speak a certain dialect, which is only a spoken language and not a written one. Experts can actually pretty much tell from which region you're from just by listening to your accent. I wasn't an expert but could still tell that they came from somewhere around Zürich.

When I told them about our boat trip and seeing the dolphins that morning, they got very excited as they both really loved animals. She wanted to become a marine biologist and go help save endangered species, and he was studying to be a vet. We started an intensive discussion about animals, and the importance of treating them with the respect they deserve.

"Unfortunately, I don't have much experience with animals, except for the lovely cat I had in our hippie-commune at home, and the cows my grandparents used to have before they had to give up the farm. I had left my cat with the girl who took over my room," I told Peter and Sue. "I often felt like I could talk to her and tell her anything, she was never in shock, but listening attentively." She seemed to like that: "The best thing you can do, if you have an animal around, is to just lay down beside them and talk to them, as you would to a very close friend. The world may think you're crazy but most of them wouldn't listen with such intensity, love and understanding....as animals do. "

"Animals have souls, and therefore feelings and I believe they are much smarter than mankind generally thinks of them", Peter continued. "That's why I want to help them." 'Here was another one who knew what he wanted to do', I thought. But since such comparing wasn't really productive, I laid that thought aside. "I think it's great when people feel called to help animals. Too many people just don't care, and are treating them like second or third class citizens on earth. Therefore we have more and more endangered species", Sue said. She was certainly right about that.

"Yep", Peter continued, "but humanity doesn't even treat other human beings with kindness and respect. That's what we're here to learn, and why we went on this trip", Peter continued. "If someone learns to treat other people with love, he will also be kind to animals." And Sue added: "The hippies don't have all the answers but at least they are questioning society's traditions and the way animals and nature are being treated. That's why we have chosen to become hippies ourselves." 'How come I hadn't met these folks at home', I thought; they are quite deep. I reflected on how many cool and spiritual people I had met since being here. This must be a special place where so much good energy gathers, I thought to myself.

I suddenly remembered that Anne had wanted to do something special with me tonight, so I helped Peter and Sue get settled in one of the stone circles, and headed over. Anne was still deeply lost in her book. "I'm back in case you still want to do something together". I told her about the couple I had just met. "Yes, Bernardo, we are getting to know so many sweet and spiritual people on this trip. This gives me so much hope that in spite of the world being so cold, there are still a lot of very warm-hearted, helpful and kind individuals in this world.""Yes, Anne. And I like people who want to help animals." Anne smiled at me: "Bernardo, if only humanity could learn to love, like we and others want to. To love people and animals and nature, and to have deep respect for other living beings. Everyone suffers pain and everyone needs compassion. I want to live a compassionate life!"

"Anyway, I do really want to spend some time with you away from the crowd. We have been talking a lot to new friends lately, but I would like some time just talking to you alone."

When Love Is Strong

S o soon we were walking through the sand dunes with the green bushes growing on top. There were a few small paths carved out, as people had walked through there before, and sometimes one would arrive at some small openings covered in sand, some of which were used by people to sleep there at night. Eventually, we found a nice spot close to the sea, and just lay down in the sand and looked up at the stars. We saw two beautiful stars falling right then. "Dou you think the second one is chasing after the first one? That would be so lovely", Anne said, while snuggling up to me. She was wearing a green, silky, oriental blouse with a matching long skirt. I started to caress her hair and whispered in her ear: "So glad you enjoyed this day, it was indeed fabulous." She looked into my eyes and slowly pulled my head towards hers, pressing her salty lips softly against mine, and I could feel her hands caressing my hair and my neck.

In the following moments, I thought I lost all sense of space and time. Our tongues met like flames of fire; it was like falling into a volcano. My head nearly exploded, as I started caressing her face and kissing her eyes. "Bernardo, I really like you. I like you a lot." I didn't say anything, but to me, her voice was like a mix of some of the best Pink Floyd pieces, especially 'The great gig in the sky'.

"I'm just scared of getting hurt again," she whispered. "Yes, so am I. But I think you're a good woman." She sat up: "Yeah? And who told you that!" She looked really surprised. "I've heard it from two sources: Once, in the morning from the waves, and then again from Claire later on." She looked at me in wonder. "And the same voice from the waves told me to be good to you. So it doesn't seem to me like anyone here wants to hurt you". She started kissing me even more passionately. "Bernardo, you are incredible." Well, I didn't think I was, but it was nice to hear anyway.

For the first time I got the feeling that some of the things I had gone through had helped to open my spiritual eyes, and had made me stronger; maybe also more dependable and a bit wiser as well. I felt a bit more like being on her level now, whereas in Formentera I had definitely felt out of her league. "You have changed a lot, Bernardo. You have found a personal connection and it has given you a lot more peace". It started getting rather chilly, so we decided to head back to our sleeping bags. "I will find out if there is a way that I can create and sell jewelry here, Bernardo. If we start having some income, we could rent a place where it's a bit warmer at night." — "But I don't want you to be the only one to bring in some cash; I must find a way to earn some too, Anne." This was still worrying me a bit, even though I had gotten some spiritual guidance regarding that in the morning.

I was mainly concerned that Anne wouldn't feel like I just wanted to live off the money she would make. "Look, Bernardo. First of all, this will be no work for me, it's my hobby. And second, I do know you're not a lazy guy who just wants to live off of others. And third, your time will come!" Once again, something I heard for the second time today; once from the waves, and now from her. It had been a truly amazing day.

The following day was when Anne had planned to go back to visit Maria. Perhaps I could go with her, I mentioned. "Would you really?" "Yes, of course, it sounds interesting." Ben and Claire were going to gather some information, finding out about schedules for their trip over to Tenerife and catching a flight from there back to Germany. "We're going to be sad to see you leave". Each one of us could have said that. We had grown quite close in those few days, through our various discussions and the boat adventure the day before. Anyway, we agreed to meet that night.

"We could try to hitchhike," Anne suggested. So we did, and the first car to pass stopped and took us up to 'El Guro'. I was thinking that I would never forget the name of this village, as it sounds just so much like a 'guru'. Some hippies had moved there after living in the caves and at the beach. A local farmer drove us straight to Maria's house, which was very sweet of him. He lived higher up in the valley and was making goat cheese. "You should visit my farm sometimes and see how I make the cheese", he said. It's nice when one can live like that and have some real 'farmer blood', I thought. It makes one quite independent from this materialistic society.

Maria was a bubbly Spanish girl, with curly light brown hair. She reminded me a bit of Janis Joplin, with her dress, with all the various things hanging around her arms and neck, but mostly with her wild and free attitude. Her house and workshop looked like a hippie-museum, with all kinds of stuff hanging on the walls, none of which seemed to have been imported, except a poster of Jimmy Hendrix and one of Janis Joplin. Maria wasn't actually from here. She had grown up in Madrid, and when the hippie-movement arrived in Spain, she had decided to move down to where the world seemed to still be somewhat intact.

She offered us some coffee, and showed us the terrace which was just absolutely gorgeous. It had this wooden veranda covered with flowers, and with some stairs going down to a beautiful garden with palm trees and all kind of vegetables growing. "In the back I also have a couple of avocado trees and a papaya tree as well", she said happily. After we chatted a bit, the girls went to the workshop while I was staying on the terrace and enjoying the view. You could see right down to Valle del Rey and further out to the Atlantic Ocean. 'It would be nice to live in some place like this', I thought to myself.

Once in a while Anne would call me in to show me some things in the workshop that had impressed her. She was able to get some beads which Maria had made from clay. "She gave me a special price," said Anne with shining eyes. "But I need to paint them myself, which is exactly what I had in mind." She was like a little girl who had found the toys she had wanted for so long. She bought some acrylic paint from Maria, as well as some leather cords, so that she would now be able to create her bracelets and necklaces without having to come to Maria's workshop. Maria would also produce more clay beads in the future if Anne needed them. So things looked quite positive that day, and we went back to our camp in good spirits. "I'll start out with this, and we'll see how it goes", Anne said. "Maybe later on I can put some black volcanic stones in between. Maria said she knows someone who cuts them."

Ben and Claire had checked out their travelling possibilities and ticketing. "We're leaving in four days", they said with a bit of a sad look. "Let's go out for dinner tonight. I'll invite you", Ben said. "Our discussions with you and Anne have been so interesting and very beneficial for Claire and me. We had just discussed this morning how meeting you both has been the highlight of our whole trip. The things we have been discussing have helped us a lot in shedding light on various issues." Anne smiled: "Well, it's definitely been the same for us. Bernardo and I have also been reflecting a lot on the different things we've been talking about," I added: "I agree with Anne. It's definitely been the best part of our trip as well. None of us know all the answers, we're far from that; but if we're open and willing to listen to the experiences of others we can definitely extend our horizon a whole lot."

After a 'siesta', we all got up and walked leisurely over to 'Playa Maria'. "Let's try 'Yaya' tonight," Claire suggested, we'll invite you." Yaya was, at that time, a beach restaurant made of wood and the leaves of palm trees. It was down at the beach, just far enough from the waves so that they wouldn't reach it. We'd heard from other hippies that the food was excellent there, and indeed it was. The sun was still quite high, and it would probably be another good hour until sunset, but we were hungry. 'Yaya' was practically next to 'Casa Maria', where the hippies would gather to drum every night. The ones who had been drumming on 'Playa del Ingles' had left in the morning, so we were looking forward to hear some rhythm here tonight.

The Long And Winding Road

"So what do you think is the right road to travel on, Bernardo?" Claire wanted to know. Well, I would have liked to know that from her, but I guess in this case it wasn't 'ladies first', so I attempted to put some of my thoughts into words. "Well, some say that following a certain ideology, spiritual path, or religion is the right way to go. It's everyone's right to do so. I'd been into several things and they all had their value. I haven't come to any conclusions though, maybe I never will, but I just think people should not be judged for the road they choose to take."

"And regarding us hippies looking for something different than this materialistic society, I think that in essence it shouldn't be that difficult to understand hippies: We just don't like too many rules, too much industrialisation, too much religion and some of us don't like too many gurus to lead us around. And we surely don't like wars and the destruction of nature and mother earth and its resources. We actually do think about the future, even though we live in the 'now'.

What we do like is friendship and getting along, and a certain amount of spirituality. We like peace and love on earth. That shouldn't be that difficult to understand."

I was always interested to see the reactions to deep thoughts that came from within, so I was looking at Claire. I could see understanding in her eyes and that made it even easier to open up about such things. "I think so too, Bernardo. I see it quite similarly. I've been reading lots of books, spiritual books, religious books, and philosophies. One thing I have found is that when something gets too rigid, like: 'This is the truth and nothing else is', then it creates a conflict inside of me, as I don't like to be boxed in. It's good to be dedicated to something, but some people take this to extremes and won't tolerate other opinions anymore. What do you think, Anne?" She looked at Anne, wondering what Anne thought about this.

Anne looked out over to the sea into the far distance. It had been that same kind of look on her face that had brought my attention to her in the first place. "I was with this Jesus group for a while. I do like Jesus and what he said, but the group had so many laws, and was so much into thinking that they had the only truth, that they didn't seem to be open to other people's experiences at all. They were always trying to talk everyone into believing their way, instead of letting people have their own spiritual experiences."

Ben had been quietly listening to all this. "What's bugging me about this issue is that people sometimes get too close to the trees so that they can't see the forest anymore. I experienced this with a guru I was following for a while up in Germany. There was a lot of truth in his ideology, and I benefitted in many ways. But I don't want to follow just one guru and the tradition they establish. I would like to be open and listen to other ideas and experiences. I don't want to just follow another man's spiritual journey; I want to walk my own."

I really liked what Ben said; it reminded me of the time I had followed a guru as well. "But if one really wants to learn from others, one can find a bit of a guru inside of everybody. I always think that anyone who knows something I don't is somewhat of a guru to me. Even the electrician who comes to the house to fix a broken line knows a whole lot more about that problem than I do." Anne smiled: "You're being very simplistic, Bernardo, but you're right. It's always good to have a meek attitude and appreciate things that other people know of, that we don't."

'Organized religion versus spirituality', that's what you could have tagged this discussion. "I do have a bit of a problem with people who get so intensely involved with a religion that they suddenly shut down all contact with people who believe differently," Anne continued. "It closes one up too much, and I don't find this helpful in an ongoing spiritual search" Claire had been attentively listening to all this, and she said: "Not every source has clean water, but we should be able to find out which one does. And if we do happen to find some clean water, we need to abstain from judging others who aren't drinking from the same source. They all should decide for themselves."

"That probably goes under respect and tolerance, which is often lacking between certain religions". I said. "When people do happen to find clean water to satisfy their spiritual thirst, it's okay if they want to tell others about it in their excitement. But I wouldn't see it as my duty to try to go around convincing everyone else. People should be trusted to be able to do a bit of searching on their own, and if they are sincere, they will certainly find the way which is best suited for them."

Ben nodded and said: "That's true, I prefer spiritual people who do not throw their weight and their words around in an attempt to try to convince others of what they believe in. That turns me more off than on." Claire agreed: "If religions can't promote kindness, tolerance and understanding in this world, then there must be something wrong with that religion, or at least with the way it's being portrayed and carried out."

Our discussion was so interesting that we almost forgot about how good the food and the 'sangria' tasted, until we started hearing the first couple of drumbeats near us. A crowd of tourists were watching as a few hippies had started with their sunset beats in front of 'Casa Maria'. Slowly, the sun started to set, and the lights were switched on outside where we were sitting. It was a beautiful scene, with the waves splashing on the right, the hippies drumming on the left, and the sun setting in the middle.

On the way back, Anne leaned her head against my shoulder, and I put my arm around her. It happened so naturally, and we smiled at each other. "This was such a beautiful evening. I really enjoyed all we talked about. It helped me see a lot of things clearer", said Anne. "It was that way for me too, Anne, I especially liked the part when Ben talked about gurus. Do you know that when I met you in Formentera, I actually considered you a sort of guru? The things you told me at that time had made a tremendous impact on me. They still do, but at that time you seemed way ahead of me spiritually.'" Anne smiled: "I'm learning so much from you right now, Bernardo. And together we learn from others as well, I think this is the right way to go."

I could feel her snuggling up to me and felt that she was enjoying it. We stood on the hill overlooking the sand dunes of 'Playa del Ingles', and I pulled her close to me and kissed her. I could feel the emotions rise in both of us, and my heart started racing. "I really, really like you, Anne", I said while running my fingers through her hair. "I feel the same way, Bernardo. At first it was friendship, but now it's more; it's been growing fast over the last days. I always liked you, but after breaking up with Pierre I needed time alone. And I was also testing you to see if you were just after sex or if you really loved me. That's why I was waiting with getting romantic, not because I didn't want it. I wanted it so many times. I'm glad you waited, that is so incredible."

"Let's go skinny dipping! We haven't been inside the water the past couple of days", I suggested. Now, as mentioned before 'Playa del Ingles' was not the ideal place for swimming at all. There were various stories going around of people who went in, 'stoned' or not, but couldn't come back to shore because the waves were too strong and pulled them back out to sea. But tonight the sea was quite calm. We weren't about to take any risks; neither of us were the kind who were going risky places, nor doing dangerous things for a thrill. After taking off our clothes, we both went in rather slowly, as it had cooled down quite a bit after sunset. She swam up to me and put her arms around my neck. I couldn't see much of her, as the moon was hiding behind the mountain. The stars shed little light, but I could still see the warmth of her eyes, accompanied by the heat of her lips as she kissed me. It was the first time I had my hands on her body, as I pulled her closer to me. The feeling of actually pulling her close and feeling her soft body was incredible. I felt like the universe was watching with great pleasure.

Holding her so close in the water felt somewhat like holding a mermaid in my arms. My hands explored her body, and I could feel her enjoying it, and I heard her whisper in my ear. "This is so nice, Bernardo...", and this encouraged me even more to touch different parts, which I so much wanted to feel. We didn't stay in the water for long, as it was quite chilly, and we sort of hurried back to our stone circle where our towels were. "We should rearrange our sleeping situation, Bernardo. Why don't we put down the towels on the sand to lie on and open both of our sleeping bags, using them as blankets. It will be a lot warmer like that at night," she said with a twinkle in her eyes. Of course, I didn't mind that idea at all. I felt my blood rushing through my head at the thought of feeling her body so close.

We continued kissing and melting into each other's arms. I kissed her ears and neck and whispered: "I've fallen in love with you, Anne." "And me with you", Anne said, and continued: "I could tell you did. You seemed like you were having a bit of a rough time the other night after I had been out with Bill." I looked at her. So she had noticed. "I tried so hard not to show it. I didn't want to make you feel bad about having been out with Bill. But yes, that day turned out to be a bit difficult for me, and made me realize that I had fallen in love." She looked at me, and I could feel that she would never judge me for it. "We're all human, Bernardo; maybe some other time it will hit me. It almost did tonight, because I could see how much Claire likes you." —"I like her too. She is similar to you in many ways, and is also deep and mature. I really like both of them and they are a terrific couple. I hope we can stay friends with them, even though they will be leaving soon."

I started kissing her shoulder as she snuggled up even closer and I could feel her fingers gliding down my back. It sent shivers through my body, and my mind was drawn into a wild spin of emotions. My lips went over her neck and down to her beautiful nipples, which I had already caressed before, when we had been in the water. I can't remember if I actually heard her whispers or if I just felt them, it didn't matter. It was like we had gotten into a big wave which was splashing us around in dreams of weightlessness. As I slowly entered her, I was suddenly lost, with nothing to hold on to but her warm body, and nothing to think about but feeling her emotions; nothing to look forward to except staying in her loving arms forever. The only thing I could hear; and I don't remember if it came from far away, or from so very near, was "Bernardo...Bernardo...I love you...."

Softly caressing, we were lying in each other's arms and, for what seemed like an eternal moment, I was gazing in silence at her amazing eyes. "This is so

beautiful. I've never felt so close to anyone, Bernardo."
I felt the same. I'd certainly never been so much in
love. It was the perfect mix of infatuation, friendship,
respect and admiration. "I've grown so close to you already, Anne. It was so beautiful tonight. I feel like it
has brought on an even higher level of intimacy. I had
been hoping all along that this would happen." We
started talking about past relationships, and in what
way this was different. We both realized how special
this was with us; like a miracle. We finally drifted off
into a peaceful sleep.

Wise Men And Gurus

The next morning Anne was up early and when I got up, she was already sitting there painting her first beads. Seeing her in action I noticed how talented and creative she really was. "Good morning, Bernardo. I just couldn't wait to start; this is fantastic. I have never painted beads before. They are gorgeous! And Maria has also done a fantastic job in forming them." "You should tell her that, Bernardo. She is actually going to teach me to make them myself from clay." Fantastic colors, I thought. "What are you going to make first, a necklace or a bracelet?" Anne thought about it for a moment. "I think I will start out with some bracelets so I will soon have something to start selling. That must be the saleswoman in me, you know".

I could still very clearly see that picture in my mind of her on Formentera, as she would walk up the street with Pierre's paintings under her arm, to sell them to shops and other customers. "I'm sure you'll be able to sell them, just as you used to do with Pierre's paintings". "Well, I have a creative side, but I also have a very communicative side and like to meet people. That's why I also enjoy the selling part. Besides, we really need the money if we're going to stay here longer."

"I will keep my eyes open for any signs regarding what I should do in order to also make a bit of money", I reiterated. "Just don't worry about it, Bernardo. I've lived more off of you so far, as you have brought along more money on this trip than I did. You also have paid nearly every meal, and the food we have bought at the shop." She was right about that, but I had stopped thinking about such things. When there was money, it was there to be used for whatever needs arose. Besides that, we really hadn't been wasteful; we just needed to eat.

I went to town to get some fresh buns from the bakery, along with a little butter and jam. We invited Ben and Claire to have breakfast with us and they were very grateful. By now, Anne had finished painting her beads, and they were laying on a rock to dry out in the sun. "Since I don't have any glaze to put on them, it's important to let the paint dry well and let the sun bake it on", she said. "And thank you for bringing some breakfast, Bernardo. Last night made me quite hungry", she said with that sweet smile and a twinkle in her eye. I kissed her. "It was wonderful and unforgettable. I feel so loved. And the beads are magnificent. I especially like that mix of yellow and blue, but the red and black ones are fantastic as well." — "I will make the first bracelet for you, Bernardo, but first I'm going to let them dry."

I just loved the way she blossomed through having a chance to practice her creativity. Claire came over to sit with us: "Ben is going on another hike, this time with Peter and Sue. They're going up to see the rainforest and will take the bus up there. In case there would be no bus to bring them back later, they will just hitchhike." I thought about the rainforest which we had seen on the way here from San Sebastian. It looked so big and mysterious and I really wanted to go see it. "I'll ask Ben if they wouldn't mind me going along as well. That way I get busy too, while you work on your bracelets." Anne looked at me with her warm smile: "I would be happy for you to go along, and we can go another time together as well. Claire is staying here with me; we have lots to talk about."

So the four of us went up to the bus-station and stopped to get some mineral water on the way there, as we were quite certain we wouldn't find any in the forest. The bus ride took about forty-five minutes. The higher the bus went, the more dangerous it seemed when looking down. Nevertheless, we arrived safely and got out at 'La Laguna Grande'. Some people had mentioned that this was quite a mystical place: A very large round circle in the middle of the rainforest, an open field where nothing grows. When it rained a lot, the water would form a lake there, which would disappear very quickly each time the rain stopped.

It was so quiet when we got there, we only heard birds; there must have been thousands of them. The center of this big opening had a fairly large circle of massive stones and, next to it, an even larger one. Peter said that someone had told him that this used to be a place where witches met. A lot of light was flooding the area, and by the time we had gotten up there, the sun was already quite hot. Various paths branched off in different directions from 'La Laguna Grande'. Obviously, it was some sort of a central place. I caught myself thinking how nice it would be if one could just watch a movie and see what had really happened in this magical place throughout the ages, in order to understand things better. There was a little restaurant nearby, so we sat down for a drink. I was happy for my 'cortado leche leche', as the hot sun hat made me a bit drowsy.

Peter shared more of the information he had gotten from a local called Alberto: "He said that the witches had quite a bit of power on the island. They made people pay tribute in order to not have a bad spell cast over their lives and houses." We were all quiet for moment. I was the first one coming with a reaction: "That doesn't sound too good, if it's true. Better to cast good spells on people. Or one could just simply pray for others and their well-being." Ben sort of chuckled: "But what the church used to do wasn't that much better in making people pay cash to have their sins forgiven."

I added: "Well, some of the spiritual gurus that my friends and I followed back home; they also wanted some money before getting us to a 'higher level'. The guru asked everyone what we were willing to give up and how much. I myself had only a couple bucks on me. But this one lady, a yoga teacher who had her own yoga-school, seemed to have quite a bit. She revealed how much she had on her bank account right there in front of us, imagine! She promised them to turn the sum over if they could just help her get to the 'higher level' they offered. It turned me off that they were so much after our money."

"Bernardo", Ben said, "Whether it is witchcraft, religion or spirituality, it always depends on the motives people have in using their spiritual powers. Their intention can be pure, or they might be doing it for some other, more selfish purpose." I was thinking about that for quite a while, as we took one of those walkways that led into the lush rainforest.

Ben continued with his elaboration of witches and gurus: "Even with these stories people tell about the witches who held reunions on these stones here, one never knows what really happened. Historical information gets passed on through many generations, sometimes getting distorted and judged along the way. By the time the details get to us we may already prejudge what had happened." I smiled: "That's why I said I'd like to go back in time and see with my own eyes what had really occurred here in this mystical place."

All the sudden clouds of fog would set in at high speed, and the whole rainforest was covered in it. After a few minutes, the clouds would lift as quickly as they had appeared. Sue said: "That's why this rainforest is so lush, because fog is setting in continuously." She knew a lot about the topic, so this whole excursion was very interesting for her as well. I was still thinking about witchcraft and religion. It had left quite an impression on me, especially what Ben said: "It depends on whether their intentions are pure or not"

"Ben, a lot of hippies have been flocking to all kinds of gurus and spiritual leaders as part of their search. At one point there were so many new groups coming to our town, all offering to have the 'only truth' and going mainly after the young people. One could say that hippies are somewhat of an 'easy catch', because of our spiritual interest and openness, with many of us being very sincere in our search for spiritual truth. Unfortunately some people and groups seem to take advantage of that."

Ben pondered a while what I'd said and then responded. "What you're saying, Bernardo, is very sad, but true. But then again, everyone can go and find out for themselves what suits them. Maybe some of these groups are partially good and bad. But people should be able to decide and find their own path." - "I agree, Ben, and I don't mean to say that all spiritual leaders are bad and have selfish motives. Sometimes they may really want to help people, but then money corrupts them or the power goes to their head."

The rainforest looked so lush and green with all the trees covered in moss, including all the branches. We went along some rocks, and suddenly saw some beautiful large dark lizards, which I might have previously only seen in zoos. There were also all kinds of incredibly colourful flowers that I had never noticed in Europe before. We were glad we had taken some water with us, because there was absolutely none on the way. "There is a waterfall somewhere, but it's quite some ways from here. That might be something for another day," Peter said.

The hiking tour we had taken was about two hours long, and we didn't want to stay any longer, as we eventually needed to hitchhike back to Valle Gran Rey. Peter and Sue got a ride first. For Ben and me it took a bit longer. There was just so little traffic, which was nice, but made it a bit more difficult to hitchhike. After a while we eventually got a ride too.

An American hippie couple picked us up. They had been on the island for about a year, but wanted to soon move on to travel some more. Joe and Ruth were their names; they had rented a little place up in 'El Guro'. She was a painter and seemed to have developed a bit of a clientele among German tourists who came to 'El Guro' in search of art and handicraft, as the village was well-known for that. "We're going to leave in a couple of weeks. We're looking for someone to rent our place when we leave. The land-lords live next door and are very sweet." I was amazed. "That sounds like very good news. Ben and Claire are leaving soon, and my girlfriend and I won't stay at 'Playa del Ingles' for too long."

So Joe and Ruth decided to show us their place. It was a small house, but it had a beautiful large veranda overlooking Valle Gran Rey and the sea. Large pots with big cactuses made the veranda look very charming for cactus-lovers like me. They showed us the living-room which had a small sofa, but a large table to dine on, with six chairs. It had a small kitchen and a bathroom with a shower, a lavabo and toilet. "It's been great for us here. Domingo and Carmela, the owners, are very nice people. Their two sons have moved on to get work in Tenerife, as it's easier to make money over there, so they decided to put this little house out for rent." The place was beautifully decorated with lovely paintings of the rainforest, local flowers, cactuses, palm trees, and local houses; all painted by Ruth. "They're stunningly beautiful!" I exclaimed. Ruth looked at me with appreciation: "Well, any of the paintings I can't sell before leaving can stay here, if you decide to rent the place. We can't carry them along."

Some Think It's Just A Leaf

I was just overwhelmed by how many sweet people I had met lately. "That's so sweet of you. I will talk to Anne about this and if you don't mind, I would like to bring her up here to show her the place, I think she'll be thrilled." We agreed that if we'd come back, they could then also introduce us to the owners. Joe was helpful, and offered to drive us all the way down to 'Playa del Ingles', so that we didn't need to walk. He even stopped on the way at 'Tienda Maria' so that we could do some shopping to surprise the girls with some cold drinks and food.

When we got back, Anne must have been waiting for me, because she came running towards me and gave me this incredible warm hug. "I have a surprise for you. Close your eyes!" I really did close them even though I could hardly wait. I felt her putting something around my wrist, and I couldn't wait any longer. It was the most beautiful bracelet I had ever seen, with this mix of yellowish-bluish and some red and black beads. It was gorgeous. I threw my arms around her neck and kissed her wildly as we were standing there for a couple minutes hugging each other. We felt so close now; like two magnets which were finally able to meet. She showed me the bracelets which she had made that day. "It's ten of them, Bernardo, and I think with time I could make even more. But, before buying more beads, I want to find out how well they will sell."

Of course I told Anne everything about our excursion; about 'La Laguna Grande', and our discussion regarding the witches and religion; about our walk through the rainforest; also about Joe and Ruth and their offer. Her eyes lit up even more: "That would be fantastic! It would be close to Maria's' workshop" She seemed to like the idea of us moving up there. "And you know what? I told them that I will check with my 'girlfriend'." Anne embraced me tightly: "You did call me your girl- friend? Oh, Bernardo, that sounds so much like a commitment, I love that, and I love you so much." I just loved seeing her emotional outbursts, they made everything seem so bright.

We unpacked the food and drinks that we had brought back with us. It had been a great day so far. Later on, Anne and I discussed our financial situation, and whether or not we could afford to pay the monthly rent on that house. "One idea would be to ask the owners if they would let us live there on a month-to- month basis, without any long-term commitment," Anne suggested. "That way we can see how things develop with the selling of my jewelry." She was wise in business matters too. We agreed that we would go up to 'El Guro' the next day.

We were enjoying our sandwiches, when Claire started another discussion. "I know we've had lots of interesting topics to discuss during our time together and we've gotten very close to each other. I thought it would be nice to bring some of the points to conclusion. In other words: What are we bringing with us from these discussions, or was it all just 'hot- air'?" I'm really going to miss these guys, I thought.

"It's sort of easy to criticize the world for going the wrong direction. The question here is if we are doing anything better?" Claire always came up with these deep questions. We were all quiet for some time, but then Ben ventured out: "I think we're trying, we're discussing problems and trying to find answers. We're asking questions that aren't being discussed in most political institutions. We may not have achieved much, but at least we are asking ourselves some basic important questions. I wouldn't minimize that at all. Because the things we discuss influence our lives and make us reflect on the way we behave in this world."

We ended up talking way into the night, until we finally lay down in blissful sleep after another great day in which so much had happened. Anne told me that she also had some very interesting and helpful discussion that day with Claire, about relationships. "Because we have one now, don't we?" she asked with a hopeful look in her eyes. "Of course we do", I said with a smile. "I was suspecting you girls would have some girl talk today."

The next morning I went to organize some coffee, as usual. Anne was always very thankful and slowly got used to staying in bed until I had brought her one. We decided to leave early for 'El Guro', and since there didn't seem to be much traffic yet, we just decided to walk. When Anne saw the house she almost screamed; she was so excited. I introduced her to Joe and Ruth, and they showed us around so that Anne could see it too. I could tell right away Anne loved it.

We were brought over to meet Domingo and Carmela. They were about the same age as our parents. I was glad I had acquired a bit of Spanish in the meantime; or at least my mix of Italian with a Spanish drift. They seemed to like us. Joe translated for us when our Spanish reached its limits. The landlords said that they would be happy to have us, but hoped that we are not loud, as once they had some hippies there who had been quite noisy. We explained that we would certainly try our best to respect the quiet of this small village, and that we both appreciated the lack of noise we had found on this island. They agreed on keeping the monthly rate the same as it was for Joe and Ruth and just asked us to give a two week notice, should we ever decide to move. For right now we definitely didn't think of moving, after just having arrived in paradise.

It seemed like the money they got from renting had helped them get a few things, as their own house looked quite well furnished with a TV and a fairly big refrigerator. Domingo said that if we wanted they could put a TV in our place as well, but we declined. Both of us hadn't been into watching TV for quite some time. We sometimes asked tourists what was going on in the world lately, and that was enough for us. We were constantly meeting and talking to people and being quite busy and would have had no time for watching TV anyway.

We gave Domingo a half a month rent as a guarantee that we were really going to rent the place. Joe and Ruth would leave in a couple of weeks by the latest; they were just waiting for some wired money to arrive at the post office of San Sebastian, and they were calling there every day to see if it has arrived. "Why don't you stay for lunch," Ruth invited us. Anne was admiring the paintings Ruth had made. "They sold quite well. I sold quite a few to German hikers, and some of them had recommended me back home, so their friends came to buy some too." I noticed some beautiful long brown leaves on the table, they looked similar to huge beans, like about 40 to 50 centimeters long. Some of them were painted with beautiful patterns and looked sort of psychedelic. I asked Joe about them. "They are the pods of the carob tree; they are far bigger here than what you might have seen in the rest of Europe. I sell them to tourists. They sell quite well as they can be used as 'shakers' because of the seeds inside and also simply as a decoration. Some prefer buying them with their natural brown colour, while others buy the ones I've painted."

"They are amazing," I said. "And where do you find them?"

Joe explained that you could find carob trees at different locations around here, but mainly in the gardens of private people. He had found out that it's best to make contact with the owners on whose property they grow on. You couldn't just shake a tree for them to fall down; you would have to actually organize some kind of a ladder and go up to pick them off the tree. Suddenly, it came out of my mouth before even thinking about it: "Would you show me where those trees are?" Joe was very happy to take me around and we agreed to meet another day for that. "I might be interested to do something like you, selling these to the tourists. I am not into making bracelets and stuff, but this looks very interesting, and painting them would be fun too. And I like the fact that they can be used as shakers."

He would file them down first with sandpaper so that they would take on the paint much easier, and then use acrylic colour. Next time we'd meet we were going to paint a few of them, so that he could show me some of the patterns he used. Now it was my turn to have shiny eyes and I noticed Anne smiling at me. "I told you that your time would come". "That's true and the waves had told me that too." Ruth looked at us and said: "You guys seem to be quite spiritual. Do you also believe in 'Deja vu'?"

Dreams And Wonders

Ruth's questions triggered this big conversation about 'Deja vu' which both of them seemed to be quite familiar with. Ruth said that she had had this dream a week or so ago, that Anne and me would be walking into their house. "And I remember you asking about the leaves of the carob tree." Then Joe added: "I guess the concept of time must be a different one in the spiritual realm." Anne and I weren't quite as familiar with this theme as them; at least we had never talked about it so far. I did have some experiences in the past where I had dreams about something and later on it happened that way, or I would know what the person was going to say or do next. That's all fine to know about, I thought, as long as the people aren't going to do something bad, or no one would get hurt or nothing bad would happen to them. I was wondering what I'd do in that kind of a situation. Would I react and prevent the bad from happening if I had experienced a 'Deja vu' about it?"

After some fresh avocados and tomatoes accompanied by local goat cheese and bread, as well as some regional wine, we felt refreshed for our journey back, and thanked Joe and Ruth for their kind hospitality.

Too bad that they would be leaving soon, as it seemed they could have also become good friends. We didn't want Joe to have to drive us back, as we just wanted to stroll back while letting those things we had discussed sink in.

On the way back, Anne said that she had known in advance that we would meet; long before we did. "When I saw you coming down that road in Formentera, I was sure I had seen that situation before, either in a dream or in some other form." We didn't need to disagree about the existence of 'Deja vu'. We both had experienced it and today's discussion with Joe and Ruth confirmed that others had done so too. It was quite inspiring actually to be so open about it, as sometimes there are things happening to us in our lives which we don't really dare to talk to anyone about, in fear that some people might think we're crazy.

Along the way, we bought some fresh drinks to bring back to Ben and Claire. "I'm just happy and thankful, Bernardo, that we have found this house to move into, I like it very much". "Yes, Anne, and those carob leaves, I love them too and I think I could sell them, they're very special." We called our parents to let them know that we'll be moving into our own house, having an address and even a phone-number where we could be reached. They of course appreciated this and we realized how little it takes to have good relations with them even if living another lifestyle from what they had hoped for.

When we got back we told Ben and Claire about the house, the carob pods and about 'Deja vu'. Of course they were very open about this topic, just as we had anticipated, as otherwise we might have been hesitant to bring it up. "Ben and I saw a UFO not long ago," Claire said. Ben looked a bit surprised and a touch uneasy about this issue coming up. He obviously seemed not to volunteer talking about it, but now that Claire had brought it up, and with both Anne and me staring at them in surprise, he slowly added: "Well, yes. I don't know exactly what it was that we saw."

Now that they had four ears and four eyes on them, they knew we really wanted to hear about this, so he continued. "It was in Tenerife where Claire and I had spent a couple of days before catching the ship to come here. We had taken a morning stroll along the beach and Claire was busy studying the menu in front of a restaurant. Suddenly I saw what looked like a balloon, the kind children usually love to walk around with on a string. Except that this one didn't have a string! It was floating down over a building on the right, then towards the beach and out to the sea on my left. I noticed that it had a blinking orange light on top. 'What a fancy new toy', I thought to myself." Ben stopped for a few seconds to see our reaction, but we were looking at him like we believed it, so he went on with his description of what he had seen.

"So I continued watching that thing, as it was flying over the beach and out into the sea. It came down all the way, almost touching the water and then hovering over it in circles for about half a minute, about 50 meters off the shore. I felt like telling everyone around to look, but I just couldn't get out a sound, I felt sort of paralyzed at that moment. By this time I knew this was not a toy and all I got out was: "Claire, look!" She was puzzled about this 'emergency', but I knew if she didn't see it she'd never believe me."

"Claire, look out there at that balloon with the blinking light!" It took Claire a bit of time to locate it and when she finally saw it, the object had stopped hovering over this one spot. It had started flying off, higher and higher out over the Atlantic Ocean. It finally disappeared on the horizon." Anne and I had been holding our hands while listening to them, and we were just both in a daze. "Truly amazing!" Those were the only words Anne could get out. "Yes, it was!" Ben continued. "It seemed to have been driven by its own power from within as there was no wind that day at all." I'm so glad Ben had drawn my attention to it, so I can confirm this awesome experience.

It sounded credible; we could see and feel it in their sincerity. "I still feel hesitant to talk about this experience, but since Claire brought it up, I did." He looked at her with a forgiving warm smile. Neither Anne, nor I had experienced something similar, but we had no problem believing that this could happen, and of course we had heard of such stories before. Why should mankind be the only species in the universe with some technical knowledge? Perhaps other species might be way ahead of us. Who knows?

Ben started a discussion about it, as obviously this experience had triggered his mind on this issue: "Mankind uses its technical knowledge mainly for economic purposes. It's amazing how we can brag about having gone up to the moon, while we are not able to feed the poor and starving. One hopes that there are other species more intelligent and loving than us somewhere in this universe. That they would not spend billions to come down here visiting us if they had their own starving on their planet."

"I agree, Ben. Mankind can't even build pipelines for supplying water from countries that have plenty to those poor ones where nothing grows and people suffer hunger. But they can build oil-pipelines from remote places to supply their own energy needs. I sure wish that somewhere in this universe there were a more loving and unselfish kind of civilization."

"Perhaps when they pass by to pay a visit to us earthlings, they don't want to make a big fuss about it. That might be one reason so few people get to see them."

"You both must be special people that they let you notice them," Anne suggested. They just smiled and said that it had certainly left a big impression on them and had made them even more spiritually interested than they had already been. Claire confirmed that it had changed Ben quite a bit, and had made him more of a quiet person, more pensive, but also more loving and understanding. "Maybe they're watching me", Ben added with a smile.

When The Wild Days
Are Over

We decided with Claire and Ben we'd meet after a little 'siesta' to walk down to 'La Playa' and see where we wanted to eat, as it was our last evening together. When we got to 'Casa Maria' that evening we heard that they had some beautiful Canarian music. There were three Spaniards with guitars, a lady who was also playing some kind of a stringed instrument, as well as a guy on bongos. We got one of the last tables that were available; the place seemed to be packed. There were many tourists, but also quite a few hippies. As a matter of fact, it was generally not clear on this island who was a regular tourist and who wasn't, as there was sort of a melting pot. Even the ones who didn't look so much like hippies were people who seemed to have a background of being alternative and spiritually minded. In talking with them, one could usually find a big sympathy for the younger generation and our search for alternative life-styles.

The evening was so much fun: We drank quite a bit of 'sangria', had nice food, while absorbing the authentic music from the islands, which was full of life. What I found so nice about this music was that they weren't just singing this for the tourists as a tourist attraction, but one could feel that it was their music relating to their island and their lives, and that they would sing it even if there were no tourists around. We all immensely enjoyed the last evening together, and made sure we wrote down all the necessary addresses to keep in touch. Ben and Claire were going to wake us up the next morning before leaving, so we tried to go to sleep soon to make it up on time; at least we tried. But feeling Anne's warm body next to mine prevented us from going to sleep right away and when we finally did it had gotten a bit late.

"Bernardo...Anne...," is what I heard when I woke up. It was Ben and Claire and they had brought us some fresh coffee which they bought from the Spanish hippie. We were up right away, and had a few more minutes with them before it was time to say goodbye. "It looks like you guys have become boyfriend-girlfriend", Claire said with a big smile. We both smiled and with warm hugs and some tears in our eyes we waved to them as they disappeared over the dunes into the distance. We felt almost a bit lonely after they had left; we had grown so close to them. "I feel like we will see them again," Anne said and I couldn't help but agree with her: "They are both very special people."

Well, now that we are up, we might as well plan our day a little bit," Anne suggested. We agreed that she would give it a try with selling the bracelets she had made, while I would go up to 'El Guro' to see if I could go with Joe to find those big carob pods. We agreed to meet before sunset at 'Casa Maria'. We said a little prayer together while hugging, that things would work out successfully while we'd be apart that day. This just happened spontaneously, but from then on, we would do this quite often, especially when we felt a bit uneasy or unsure about something.

I was really hoping that it would be a good experience for Anne. I knew she had sold Pierre's paintings to tourists in Formentera and that she had the talent for this. Still, seeing her go off alone like this made me pray in my heart for everything to go well. I could have gone along with her, but we both thought I might be more in the way than of any help. As she said, she had already learned in Formentera to listen to that still small voice guiding her to the right people.

So I decided to hitchhike up to 'El Guro' and the second car that came by brought me straight there. Joe was sitting on the veranda drinking a coffee when I arrived. He said that Ruth had told him I would be coming this morning. "How did she know?" Joe smiled: "Deja vu". I thought that this was a nice and helpful spiritual gift to have, so you knew who to expect at around what time. "Does she really get these things that often?" I asked. "Almost daily," Joe answered. "But don't worry; her head isn't constantly in the clouds because of that, she is actually quite down to earth. Yesterday she was at the doctor's office as she has felt a bit sick lately, especially in the mornings. And guess what: She is pregnant!"

He could see the surprise on my face. "So this will certainly help keep her feet down on earth and I guess mine too". He seemed to be happy, so I congratulated him just when Ruth came out. She was happy about it too. "We hadn't really planned it, but now that it happened, we are both very excited. We will need to rearrange our plans though. It's not that we are not going to leave from here, but instead of going to India as we had planned, we'll return to the States." That was all big news. "Yes, Bernardo, once you get a kid, the kid comes first, and travelling to India may not be the best for him. And, besides we have seen quite a bit of the world, we have been travelling together through Europe for the past four years, including our one year stay here, so we've seen a lot." Ruth added: "We called our parents last night, and they are overjoyed and happy to help us all they can, once we're back. But don't worry, we'll stay hippies; it's in our blood."

My head was spinning with so much exciting news. For a moment, I was thinking what I would do if I were to get a kid. I mean, not me, but the person I'm with. I put that thought away for further elaboration at a later date, and for now made arrangements to go with Joe to find those trees. "They usually grow in someone's garden; they don't seem to grow wild around here. It is therefore only a matter of courtesy to ask the people whose property these trees are on, if you can take some of these pods. A little 'gift' always helps. People aren't rich here, and we cannot expect to just get everything for free, even though we are poor as well." I thought that was a good attitude to go by.

So we visited three different places. Joe introduced me to each of the people who had these carob trees. He told those sweet people I could give them the same 'gift' he always did if I could sometimes pass by to get some. At two of the places they provided a ladder and at the third place they let us go through their staircase onto the roof. The tree was growing right beside the house and it was easy to reach them from there. Joe was a real pro: He had taken a pair of garden scissors with him and clipped them off nicely. "If you don't clip them off they may rip and that would be sad. A storm might throw a few of them on the ground, but it only happens a few times a year around here."

After getting back to Joe's house with a bag full of these huge carob pods, he took some time to show me how he treats the ones he paints. "Some tourists don't want them painted as they have such a gorgeous dark brown color. Others seem to think that they're nothing special when they're not painted." He showed me the different patterns he uses and I was able to paint some myself. "I would like to take one to Anne when I go back". "They're all yours! I will leave my 'business' for you when we leave." Again I had this beautiful feeling of being so blessed in meeting so many precious people lately.

"I will also take you to a couple of shops that buy them from me. Of course, you don't get too much from them, as they also want to gain their money for selling them." I had never really sold anything in 'direct marketing', so this was going to take somewhat of a step of faith for me. But with Anne beside me, and that still small voice inside me, I felt I was somewhat ready for this.

I spent the whole afternoon there painting quite a few of them. At first I copied some of the same patterns and color combinations that Joe had used. But after I had painted a few, my own creativity started taking over. I had never been that much of an innovative person when it came to working with my hands, but I was quite happy with the results. I found it challenging to try out new variations of the patterns I was shown. I thought with time I could come up with totally different ones and not just copy Joe's.

It was getting time to leave and meet Anne. We put the painted pods to dry and I took along the first one I had made, making sure it was dry. I had put it out in the sun and the colors were shining beautifully. I thanked Joe for all his help, and we gave each other a big hug when I left. I hitchhiked down to 'Casa Maria' in order to get there faster. I could hardly wait to meet up with Anne. She was already waiting for me out on the porch, sipping on some cold lemonade. Her eyes lit up when she saw me, she looked like she had some good news as well. After the warmest hug she looked at the painted pod in my hand, and she just flung her arms around me real tight. "This is absolutely beautiful, Bernardo." It sort of reminded me of when I used to bring something home to my mom that we had made at school. I could tell Anne really liked it. "I made it for you. It was the first one I painted today. And how did things go for you?"

She then told me about all the bracelets she had sold that day. "I could have perhaps sold more, but I ran out, so I came here and was watching the waves while waiting for you. I met a nice girl from Denmark and we talked for quite a while." I was so happy things had gone well for her. Since we were both quite hungry by now, we went ahead and ordered something to eat. "And guess what, Anne. They just found out yesterday that Ruth is pregnant." - "That's so amazing, Bernardo! I do think they are going to be very sweet and loving parents."

LONELY TRAVELLER

The next days were spent with Anne working on her bracelets and on necklaces as well. They were made with the same kind of beads. Sometimes she had to go to 'El Guro' to get more material and Maria was always very helpful and let her work there at the workshop. Anne also started attending the yoga workshops at Maria's house. After a few days of going to Joe and Ruth's place, I felt like I had enough of those carob leaves painted, and I was hoping that I would also muster up enough courage to go and sell them now. Maybe I was trying to put that off a bit.

In my bag there were about twenty-five of these carob pods, some painted and others not. I wanted to just find a permanent place where I could display them, rather than walking around having to unpack my merchandise each time to try to sell one to an individual. Close to 'Casa Maria' I sat down on the wall in front of the beach. Anyone coming from either direction had to pass by there. After unfolding Anne's nice Nepali drape I put out all my carob pots orderly and I thought it looked really cool. I had seen some other hippies selling stuff there before, that's how I had gotten the idea.

Anne had gone up to 'El Guro' to see Maria and we were going to meet here again that evening. It was a lot of fun sitting there with people stopping and looking at my pods. Most of them were very surprised to see such huge carob pods. They hadn't seen such large ones of these beautiful leaves before, just like I'd never seen them either before coming here. Things went quite well I met many interesting people from all over the world.

When Anne came back from 'El Guro', I was already waiting for her over a cold beer, as I was thirsty and needed a drink. I had sold fifteen of my pods and was very happy about it. We ordered a bottle of wine to celebrate, as well as some food with it. Not having a kitchen used up quite a bit of our money, and so we were looking forward to move into our small house soon.

So that's how the days went by, until Joe announced that they had made travel arrangements for the coming weekend. They would fly from Tenerife to Madrid, from there to London, and then onward with a direct flight to New York. Again some dear friends would be leaving. I had gone a few times to their house recently, and sometimes Anne came along after being at Maria's. We continued having many good conversations with them. They both were a few years older than us, but that didn't matter at all; we felt very comfortable around them.

On the same day that we were going to move, Anne and I had gone for some warm breakfast to 'Yaya', as for some reason we had missed out on dinner the night before. When we got back to the beach, all our stuff was gone. We looked everywhere, but it had disappeared! We asked the few people that were around if they had noticed anything. Peter and Sue who had taken over the stone circle beside us, the one Ben and Claire had been in before, had left a couple days earlier. Until then, we had always been watching each other's things a bit, making sure that no one would go through any of our personal belongings. But we hadn't gotten to know anyone else closely since then, as we were quite busy learning to earn a living.

LONELY TRAVELLER

We were thankful though, that it was only material things that had disappeared, mainly our clothes, sleeping-bags and backpacks, and in a way we knew we were risking that by living at the beach. Our documents and all our money we always had with us, so we still had all that, thankfully so.

Metamorphosis

So we arrived empty handed at Joe and Ruth's place that afternoon. "Maybe it's sort of a sign that your time at the beach was up," Ruth said. We were sure glad to be able to move into a place with a stove, fridge, bed, toilet, shower, running water and electricity. Joe and Ruth were going to take the evening bus, spending the night in a pension in San Sebastian. We helped them with any last minute packing, though there wasn't that much left to do. "I have sold three more of my paintings recently, but I give you the ones left", Ruth said. "The household stuff mostly belongs to Domingo and Carmela. Any perishable stuff you find in the fridge is all yours." They were just so sweet; sometimes I think they must have been angels. Joe turned his whole workshop on the veranda over to me. He had left the big bag of carob pods there and so I had enough for a while. Later on we helped them bring their suitcase to the bus and after hugs and some tears, we waved them goodbye.

That had been another busy and exciting day. Not all positive, but it could have been a lot worse. The things we had lost were all replaceable. We were a bit sad that such good friends had left again, and of course, we had decided to stay in touch by exchanging addresses, now that we had one as well.

Anne was cooking some spaghetti with fresh tomatoes and grated cheese she had found in the fridge, and we just relaxed from this somewhat hectic day. As we lay in each other's arms that night, we were really thankful for having been protected from real harm. We also said a little prayer for dear Joe and Ruth to have a good journey back to their home country and a good start into their new life.

"Amazing to think that they are going to have a baby", Anne said. "I'm sure they'll be good parents; they have a lot of love for others." For a moment I could almost hear Anne add: "We would make good parents too", but I don't think she really said that. So far we had generally believed that we didn't want to have any kids. 'The world has gotten so bad that we don't want to bring more kids into this world' had been a common belief among many hippies in those days.

Things went well for us once we had gotten settled into our little house. We were able to get some hippie-clothes at the shops in exchange for some bracelets and carob pods. We didn't hear the waves anymore, as we were now higher up in the valley, but we went down to Valle Gran Rey almost daily to sell some of our stuff or to do some shopping. Life wasn't quite that wild anymore, as we settled into our new home and found a certain amount of stability. Anne's creations were getting more beautiful all the time and she made some really amazing stuff, with some pieces of real silver in between, as she just wanted to make sure people got good quality products from her.

I personally felt that selling those pods from the carob tree wasn't going to be like the ultimate trip for me, but at least it offered some way to make a bit of money for now, and I enjoyed painting and selling them. I also got to know a lot of interesting people from all over the world whom I'd gotten into conversations with. Since this wasn't a place for mass tourism, almost every person I met was in some way special, either by being interested in spiritual stuff or with some kind of alternative or ecological interests.

One time, there was an older lady from Switzerland, who stayed exceptionally long at my 'street-shop' talking to me. I had told her I had a girlfriend, but that didn't pose a problem for her. So she kept coming to see me daily while on holiday. I told Anne about it and also about her invitation to go with her to 'see her room' at the pension she was staying at. "That's sweet of you to tell me, Bernardo. I can get jealous easily if I feel insecure, but your honesty really helps." I did go for a drink with that lady a couple times at 'Casa Maria' as she was very kind and we had some good talks. Anne naturally had similar encounters with men who were interested in her. It was good that we started being very open to each other about such things at an early stage of our relationship.

We started participating at the weekly market that had opened at the bus station and were able to rent a table there for selling our stuff each weekend. Other hippies would be selling paintings, self-made Aloe-Vera products, home-made jam, fruit and vegetables from their gardens, and all kinds of jewelry. For Anne, it actually didn't go that well there as there were just too many hippies selling jewelry. With my carob pods it went a bit better at the market, being the only one selling these. They were actually quite popular with the tourists as they look so naturally beautiful.

We got enough money to pay the rent and to get ourselves lots of fresh fruit and vegetables from some of the hippies in our village, who were selling their home-grown avocados, tomatoes, mangos papayas, salad etc. Soon we knew practically all the hippies that were permanently living around Valle del Rey.

So life went on, and we lived our lives at that little house in 'El Guro'. We couldn't hear the waves, but we could still watch them from up there as they were approaching the shore. We could see the sun glittering on top of the Atlantic Ocean in the late afternoon, and enjoy the variety of sunsets on the horizon each evening. We could hear hundreds of birds singing as we woke up each morning. Besides selling our jewelry and carob pods, Anne kept attending the regular yoga meetings at Maria's and she continued to make a lot of progress. I would often find her in a certain yoga-position on our terrace when coming home, and it was always such a gorgeous sight, especially if the sun would set simultaneously. Now that we felt more secure with each other we had found peace.

We had gotten settled in our new situation as well as in our relationship, when Anne threw up one morning. I tried to figure out what it could have been, but we hadn't eaten anything different. She got better, but two days later she felt quite dizzy again after getting up. I started getting a bit concerned, so that day I went with her to see the doctor down in Valle del Rey. I was waiting outside, and hoped it would not be anything serious. When Anne came out, she said, with shiny eyes: "Bernardo, I'm pregnant!"

I wasn't too sure if this was better news than a sickness, but in some ways it probably was, judging by the light on her face. On the other hand it was like a great dam had just burst up on the mountain, and the water was now gushing down on me. "I don't have a serious income, Anne...," was the first thing that came out. I think I lost a bit control, because that certainly must not have sounded very encouraging for her. Nevertheless, she smiled and said: "Bernardo, look. That small voice has led us each step of the way, and it's going to continue to lead us now." 'Young hippies having a child', I thought, 'that must happen more and more as the original teenage hippies were getting older. Is there a book on how to handle this?'

I was aware of the fact that people usually burst out into major screams and shouts after such news, and everyone congratulating, 'normal' people that is. I guess I wasn't 'normal' enough, because to me it brought along a whole set of new questions that added to all the ones I had already had regarding having children. First: this world was not getting any better, but worse, so anyone having children must not have been aware of this. And second: It's a fact that children would cost a lot of money. And Anne and I were just barely making enough to live on our own.

This was the sort of wave I was hit by, but Anne just smiled and looked so happy. What had happened to her? Before she would have understood and agreed with my points, but now that she had found out she was pregnant, she suddenly felt like it was all okay to have kids. 'On the other hand', I thought, 'you must

understand her too: it's not you who has gotten pregnant, and for a woman this is a very special thing; it's
her baby.' Now this was probably the first time I tried
to argue a bit with that still small voice. 'Sounds all ok,
but it's my baby too, and I will need to provide for it,
and prove myself of being a good father'. The voice
didn't say anything; it didn't seem to like to argue.

For the next two days I just sort of caved in: I
didn't argue with the voice within me, neither did I try
to make any negative comments to Anne. I had already failed to encourage her when she had come out
of the doctor's office, and I still felt bad about that. My
comment had sounded like this baby would be some
kind of a curse, being born to a father who was a hippie instead of a 'normal' member of society. The baby
was going to be born to a 'freak'. But entertaining such
thoughts didn't really help me any further, so I decided I was going to have to find the brakes.

So the next morning it was meditation time for
sure, with somewhat of a less pleasurable approach
this time, as I didn't know what that still small voice
was going to tell me at this point. This time I wasn't
hearing the waves, just a few birds. As I shut down my
thoughts and worries, I could hear that little voice
again inside me: "Listen to Anne." I heard it quite
clearly and I didn't want to argue, but thought about
it. Before letting out any more of my negative comments, it would make sense to listen to her view of
things. We were in the same boat. Then I realized how
much Anne had given me, in spiritual strength, trust
and love. She had brought so much joy into my life
and we made such a good team.

My whole ideology had been centered on love, and that we should love and respect each other, the animals as well as nature. So here was a new human being formed right next to me; our own son or daughter. I felt like my whole ideology, everything that I believed in, was now being put to test.

"Anne, I really need to talk to you," I said as I entered the bedroom that evening. She was lying in bed and writing a few things in the diary she had started after she had seen mine. Well, mine wasn't really a diary, just a collection of thoughts and things, but she took this a lot more seriously and had started to write into her diary each evening. I had wondered what she was writing in there , but I didn't want to be too curious, as every soul deserves some privacy.

"I'm sorry for the comment I had made after hearing the news of the pregnancy. It must not have been very encouraging to you. I just was so totally unprepared for this." She looked at me with eyes that expressed so much understanding. "It is okay, Bernardo. We went on this trip together to look for a better world, for new realities. We hadn't anticipated that this might include a baby. When the doctor told me about it, my walls inside just collapsed. I felt that I didn't want to let a corrupt and messy world take away my chance of being a mother and experiencing the joy of having a baby. I know we used to always say that the world is so bad, that we wouldn't want to bring any more kids into it. But there is a life outside of society, even if we have to live in the midst of it." She had a point. Why should we let a selfish and materialistic society and its destruction of mother earth discourage us from having children? Of course the world didn't seem like it would get any better and future generations will probably have it even more difficult. But I also came to the realization that this doesn't need to necessarily stop us from raising children.

It's not easy these days to live in this world: On one hand we disagree with so much of what's being done to people, to animals and to nature. On the other hand we can't build a new society as they wouldn't let us. So we have this society we don't like with all its rules and regulation that we have to live by, while somehow make enough money to survive. We have to adapt to this society whether we like it or not, because it is stronger. But in our hearts we can still live by the principles of our own society built on love. There is still no law in this world that forbids us to be loving and peaceful.

"Bernardo, a bit later the thought crossed my mind that perhaps you'd want me to abort it." She had this look on her face that was at the same time sad but also with hope that I wouldn't consider such a thing. "Well, I hadn't really thought about that, but it would not seem to go along with my whole ideology of love. How could I agree to destroy a life that's growing right next to me when I believe in love, respect and peace? I guess my main worry is the financial support as we're neither regular members of society nor having a steady income." "I know, Bernardo, I've been thinking about that too. But we are not the poorest of the poor and I believe that having children should not be just re-served for the rich." She hit the nail right on the head.

"Well, Anne, I do understand people who need to abort because they just don't think they can provide for the child or whatever other legitimate reason they may have. But in a way, I do think I have enough faith that we will get enough money to get by. We have already been able to make some money while being thousands of kilometers away from home. I just needed some time to find peace about it and my meditation time this morning really helped with that, as the spiritual energy seemed to indicate that I should listen to you. I will do all I can to help provide for you and the child, even if it may include some hard work. You both deserve my help and support in any way possible. This is all so new for me, but I want to take on the challenge of being a good daddy." Anne took me into her arms and caressed my face and started kissing me gently. Later on we kissed more desperately and had another one of so many beautiful love-sessions that helped us forget all our problems and cares.

The next morning as I sat down to meditate some more about this new situation I felt so much peace. I wanted to have this child too, I had accepted and agreed to this new turn in our lives. My only concern now was the financial aspect and how I might be able to make more money in order to provide for this additional passenger that was soon going to be added to our team. 'I want to take you to another level'. There it was again. It wasn't so clear to me what that was supposed to mean, but while talking to Anne about it later on, it became a lot clearer.

I told Anne: "Well, sweetheart, maybe it's time for us to bring our financial support base to a higher level, taking another big step just as we did when we left society behind and went to look for something else. We had hoped that things would work out, and they did. Now comes another step of faith and we can hope that this time things would work out too, and they probably will." Her eyes lit up as this seemed this encouraged her. "I love you so much, Bernardo, you seem to have a spiritual connection that allows you to see beyond natural circumstances." Well, it certainly seemed to do me some good to meditate and pray, instead of listening to all my fears about the future.

Anne came up with an idea: "I saw some hippies with kids here. I used to make a bit of a circle around them, as this wasn't my idea of living; I wanted to travel more. They also seemed a bit older than us, but now we're starting to get older too." She looked thoughtful for a few seconds. "Maybe we should talk to some of them. Apparently they are still hippies, you can see it on their faces and in the way they dress, and even in the way they dress their kids, so cute."

"Maybe the hippie girls who are already having kids might be able to give me some tips for my pregnancy. I just really have no idea." For the first time I saw how helpless she was too; I wasn't the only one who was puzzled. "And maybe I can look into finding a couple of books about pregnancy and childbirth. I would really like to know more about it. And we just need to get used to the idea that we won't be so wild and free anymore; that there is going to be someone entering our lives that requires some stability and a certain amount of security."

I could really see the mother instinct awakening inside of her. In this new situation she seemed to look at things a lot more pragmatically than I did. My admiration grew for her, as I could see her making the turn from being a young, wild and free teenager, to a responsible young adult. Someone who took the responsibility for what lie ahead of her.

"Anne, I'm sure we can have a child and still remain hippies. After all, this does not need to change our whole ideology and beliefs." I guess it was a mix of listening to Anne and to that still small voice which had given me new faith and hope for this situation. "I wasn't planning on selling carob pods for the rest of my life anyway" I said. "We wouldn't be the first hippies to leave this hippie paradise out of necessity." "Yes, Joe and Ruth were also confronted with pregnancy, and from what I heard there are quite a few others as well. We just received a letter from them this morning and they wrote that they have settled down, and she is learning a lot about her pregnancy. They are sending lots of love and missing us." I just lay down, and put my arms around her, and we both felt that things were going to be okay somehow. We had found peace about this new situation.

Anne actually really started talking to hippie mamas whenever she would meet one and was gathering information about pregnancy. Most of the ones she talked to had been here before but had gone to mainland Europe or to Tenerife to have their baby. For certain nationalities the governments would only pay the hospital fees if you were giving birth in your home-country or at certain clinics. I was hit with lots of new details almost daily and after a while I felt almost like I was going to become a pregnancy expert.

During my times of meditation and prayer, which I usually took in the mornings, I started facing the fact that I was going to have to find some other means of support. That posed a real challenge for me and so I was really looking for some guidance, which I didn't seem to get right away. Anne continued with her jewelry production and started going for regular visits to the doctor's to check that everything with the baby was okay. I started asking around a bit and found out from quite a few sources that some hippies had gone over to Tenerife once they had kids. There was much more tourism there and it was apparently easier to make money. I specifically addressed this issue one morning in meditation and prayer, and there it was as clear as ever. 'There is something new for you'. I didn't hear what, but everything went sort of step by step in my life, it didn't all come served on a silver platter.

With My Guitar On My Back

I think it was a day or so later when I was over at Domingo and Carmela's house paying our monthly rent, when I saw this beautiful Spanish guitar hanging on the wall in the corner. I used to have a similar one, but when I left Switzerland to go on this trip with Anne, I had sold it to Monica as we just couldn't travel with so much stuff. "This guitar is from my son, but now he's in Tenerife working as a waiter and he doesn't use it." I hadn't even asked about it, but Domingo was quite a spiritual man too. "Do you play?" he wanted to know. "Well, I haven't been playing for a while, Domingo, but it would be nice sometimes to see how much I remember." Then he looked at me and said: "You can take it over so you can use it anytime you want. That's better for it than just hanging here." I was so surprised. I guess sometimes we don't need to hear voices from the spiritual realm around us about what to do. Sometimes guidance for our lives comes from things happening right there around us.

I started playing the guitar again. There was a cassette player in our house which we hadn't even really looked at. Now that I took a closer look, I realized there was a whole stack of cassette tapes beside it: Bob Dylan, Beatles, Rolling Stones, Joan Baez, Cat Stevens...It was like pieces of a puzzle were being dropped in my hands daily. I started listening to and writing down lyrics and figuring out chords. Anne was excited that I would play the guitar. She had only heard me once when she was visiting me at our hippie-commune back home. I would often practice when she went over to Maria's or was out selling jewelry. That way my practicing wouldn't go on her nerves and I could play her the songs I had learned once I really knew them well. She loved them.

I was still painting my carob pods as well, and going out to sell them, while using as much of the rest of my time to practice. Soon I had about a dozen songs together. 'There is something new for you'. Well, maybe that was it. 'Maybe I was supposed to get into music for now', I thought to myself. I wanted to talk to Anne about it, so one evening I explained to her about all the small hints I had gotten lately. She had felt it already: "I knew something was going on and I'm glad you seem to be getting some answers. I don't know where this will lead you to, but I feel you're going the right direction. Your singing and guitar playing is really good, Bernardo." She was always encouraging me even when neither of us really knew if we were going the right direction.

Things had worked out quite well financially for us during the past few months, so we were able to put a little money aside. I was thinking of getting my own guitar and told Anne about it. "Of course you should get one, Bernardo, you play so well". "That's sweet. But I don't want to just get one to play at home. I would like to get one so that I could make some money with it." Now it was her who looked surprised. "But where? At Casa Maria?" she smiled. We both knew that the sort of music I played wouldn't fit there. So I dared to say the unspeakable: "Maybe the time will come for us to move on." She looked even more surprised. "Where do you get all these ideas from, Bernardo?" I didn't really know either. Sometimes it was from that voice inside and other times from things I'd heard when asking around. "Some hippies who started having kids went over to Tenerife as there is a lot more tourism there, and more money to be made." I hated talking about 'more money to be made', but at the same time we were really facing some new and important factors. Anne was quiet for the rest of the day, but in the evening, while lying in my arms, she said: "Bernardo, I knew from the beginning that selling the carob pods wasn't entirely your cup of tea, but that you did so mostly out of necessity. I would really like to see you do something that makes you happy. Getting more money isn't the main issue."

The following day I talked to Domingo and asked him if any of his sons would know of a cheap place I could stay at for a few days if I went over to Tenerife. He said that they had landed at 'Torres Del Sol' in Los Cristianos after arriving. There are cheap apartments to rent for one week at a time. "Thank you so much, Domingo, you're so helpful to us. By the way, would you know of any music shop there in Los Cristianos?" Domingo smiled: "I know there is one. I bought that guitar there for my son while on a business-trip."

The next morning, before making any further moves in that direction, I took some time to meditate and pray. 'Go where the doors are open' is what I felt I heard this time. So I talked to Anne later on and it seemed she also felt it was time to move on, but not for both at once. In discussing things, it became quite clear that I should go there for a few days and see if I could get a guitar and look into some opportunities to play music which would generate some support. While there I could check into cheap places to land, in case we both moved over. "And," Anne added, "You could see if there were any possibilities for me selling my jewelry there." So I had quite a bit to do. I checked the schedule for the bus and the ferry to Tenerife while Domingo phoned for any vacancy at 'Torres Del Sol apartments' for me. Two days later I was on my way, with big hugs and prayers from my sweetheart. I felt like I was leaving her in good hands, as Domingo and Carmela would always ask if we needed anything when they went shopping by car. They were really helpful to us.

As we pulled into the port of Los Cristianos, one of the passengers pointed towards two towers close to the sea. "Those are the 'Torres Del Sol'". 'Not exactly a hippie paradise', I thought to myself, but for a few days it should do. When I got there, I found out that Domingo had actually not only asked for a vacancy, but had made a reservation for me, so I was glad to drop my bag in the room on the tenth floor of that huge tower. At least I could see directly over to La Gomera from there, and knew that Anne wasn't far away.

That evening I went out in hopes of finding some live-music somewhere, so I could talk to some musician and get some information about performing. I did find a keyboarder who was playing dinner music out on a terrace, and when he had a break I grabbed the chance to talk to him. "In your situation, with no equipment except an acoustic guitar, I would just go busking first. Once you busk and get to know your way around, you get to know the music scene a bit and get offers for this and for that." This sounded like a good idea, I had to get started somewhere. I decided to try this out, but first I'd need to get a guitar. I also got to know a hippie who was sitting on one of the main beachfronts where lots of people were passing by.

He was selling little trees which he made out of wire, with semi-precious stones hanging on them, which apparently sold quite well. His name was Eduardo; he was from Argentina and his wife was French. She stayed home with the kids while he was out selling his self-made trees every night. They had also been to La Gomera for some time, but when their first child was born they decided to come over here. Now they already had their second child. "You can make a bit more money here than over in La Gomera, which you need if you have kids. There is just so much more going on here, but I do miss the quietness of La Gomera and the hippie community there. Here there aren't that many."

I asked him about the possibilities of Anne selling jewelry, and he thought that this could go well. Some of their friends were also into producing and selling jewelry. "If I can sell these trees, then you can also sell jewelry. It just shouldn't look too much like hippie-style, as the majority of the tourists here are not hippies." 'Well, Anne may have to adapt her jewelry a bit to the new situation', I thought to myself. I knew she was flexible. "I'll come by here again tomorrow night to see if you're here, Eduardo. It's good to have met you, bro."

After a good night's rest at 'Torres Del Sol', I went to look for some breakfast. Everything here seemed much cheaper with so many restaurants, bars and pubs. Each of them was trying to have the lowest price to compete with the other. I just got myself some English breakfast with sausage, a couple of fried eggs, fried bacon, beans, bread and butter. The sausage was practically inedible, but the rest was okay. When I thought the shops might have opened, I made my way over to the center of Los Cristianos where I found the music shop. As it hadn't opened yet I needed to wait for a few minutes before it did. I noticed that there were so many more cars driving around here. It was probably a bit like coming from the mountains of Colorado to New York, or something like that. It just seemed so much busier over here.

The mass-tourism had set in, and literally hundreds of hotels and thousands of apartments were being built for the sun- and beach-hungry tourists from Western Europe, who were streaming in by the thousands. Such a large tourist center like Playa de las Américas and Los Cristianos (the two places have grown together), needed a lot of infrastructure and there were tons of supermarkets, restaurants, bars, pubs, discos, recreational centers and all kinds of shops everywhere.

'I don't think Anne will like it here, I don't like it either', I thought to myself and for a moment I was thinking about taking the next ferry back to La Gomera. But then I heard something inside of me saying. "'The perfect place for you is only in your heart". That was quite a bomb. I had never looked at it this way. I had always thought the perfect place to be was away from the rest of the world. I think I kept on thinking about that over the next few days, but I obviously took this into consideration during the rest of my stay there. Maybe one can live a bit outside this little Las Vegas and just come here to make some money. I remembered Eduardo had said they lived somewhere up in the hills.

By now the shopkeeper arrived, parked his car and opened the door to the music shop. His name was Ruben. He had quite a number of guitars of all sorts on display; from classical Spanish guitars to various acoustic guitars, including twelve-stringed, as well as a variety of electric ones. If I was going to go by the advice the keyboarder had given me, it would probably be best for me to get a plug-in acoustic guitar that I could use for busking, but also be able to plug into a sound-system in case I would get some more permanent assignments.

"If you are looking for an acoustic guitar, I have a nice Yamaha here", Ruben said. "I had sold it to a British singer who was using it to sing in a bar, but after about a month, his father died and he had to return to England, so I bought the guitar from him. It has been used shortly, so I could give it to you quite a bit cheaper than if it were new. It has a pick-up in case you'd need to play with an amp at some point." I looked at it carefully and saw that it had been well taken care of with no scratches. "There is a hard case for it which I'd throw in for free", Ruben said. I wanted to try it out, and so I started playing around on it. It did have a beautiful full sound, and the strings were soft on my fingers and it seemed to serve its purpose. He had some other nice ones which were brand new, but the price difference was tremendous. So I got myself the Yamaha with the case, and he also gave me a strap, some guitar picks, and a tuner for the guitar; all for the price he had agreed on. I thought I'd made a good deal, and it turned out I had.

I headed back to 'Torres Del Sol' with my new guitar which I left in my room for now. I went to a big supermarket nearby to get some food, as I didn't want to eat out in a restaurant. I was surprised how much cheaper things were over here; at least thirty percent cheaper, which could make quite a difference, when one needs to start buying diapers and other baby stuff. I wanted to call Anne that night on Domingo and Carmela's phone and inform her of the latest. By the time I called her there were lots more of exciting news to report.

New Horizon

After having made myself some lunch, I went out to see what sort of bars and pubs I could find, and perhaps make some possible contacts for singing. There were lots of British and Irish pubs around, but I also checked out some others, as I was willing to sing anywhere where they would let me. I had a little notebook, in which I wrote down information about places, the names of the bosses, phone numbers and things like that. Some places asked me to come back in the evening, as the boss would be around by then. I did get to talk to some owners, and by time the sun had set, I had about five who were interested in my songs and repertoire. "We need well-known songs that people can just sing along to, so they drink more." The general idea was that I would sing, and they'd pay me a little something, but I could also 'pass the hat'. So I needed to get some kind of a hat. I found one later that just really matched my style and personality.

I got hungry, so I went to my apartment to cook myself some spaghetti and then I called Anne. It was so good to hear her sweet voice and that she had a good day. She had been to the doctor's and he said that everything with the baby was fine. I was happy to hear that and filled her in on everything. When I told her that it wasn't so nice here with all these endless hotels, restaurants, bars, and discos, she said. "The peace we find must be within." I missed her, and felt a bit like a fish out of water, but at the same time we realized that it was good for us sometimes just having to stand on our own feet.

Anne did voice some concerns as well: "Even if for some reason we need to go and work in the city in order to make some money for our personal survival, we must do our best to stay out of the cities and in close contact with nature," Anne said. "I don't want to go to a new place and be stuck in another one of those cities we had just escaped from". "I agree, Anne. I guess that's probably why I had wanted to just return to La Gomera a couple days ago, I definitely didn't like being surrounded by all these man-made tourist bunkers." Cities for tourism instead of for industry didn't seem much better, except that people were in a better mood.

"Well, Bernardo, we have been led by an unknown voice and things have worked out by doing so. Maybe later on we might find a way to get ourselves a 'finca' and grow our own stuff and not be so dependent on the money. Money enslaves people, it makes them have to go places they may not really want to go, just for economic reason. But if we've been led that way, then maybe some door will open for us so that we'll be able to live out in nature" She was right about that. "I definitely want to, Anne. Some hippies live out of town and just come here to make some money and I hope we'll be able to do the same."

"Thank you for looking into this, Bernardo." I was quiet for a minute. The success of these last days had clouded out a bit that we mainly needed to come here for financial reasons. If money were no problem, we probably would have never done so and would have stayed in our happy home in "el Guro".

"I agree with you, Anne. We don't want to get stuck in another city and get so busy making money that we won't have time for meditation and prayer like we did have until now. That's the kind of situation we had fled from! At the same time we do need to make some more money, as we have a child coming into our lives soon. But we didn't decide to come here just for money; we actually did meditate and pray a lot about this decision. We don't know yet how this might possibly turn out to be an ever better situation."

"Bernardo, I love you so much, thank you for tuning into my concerns. I'm sure we'll find a nice place out of town there, maybe it will take a little time." I could understand her concerns. "Anne, if you agree I would come pick you up and we'll try our best to find a situation here that is away from this mass tourism. It won't be the same as it was before, but it can still be nice and peaceful and away from the crowd. And I'm sure we can find new hippie-friends here as well. I have already found one." I told her about Eduardo.

After some big hugs and kisses over the phone, I went on to sing in a couple more places and then went to sleep. I don't know if it was a good sleep, as our discussion over the phone had been quite intense. It's amazing how things can be so clear to you after meditating and praying and getting answers, and can get so muddled up when you start looking at the things happening in reality.

Later on, I passed by to talk some more with Eduardo, who was at the same place selling his stone-decorated little trees again. "It gives us enough to care for our two kids. We're quite happy here and it's not as bad as we thought it might be when we first got here. There are quite a few hippies living up in Adeje, which is not directly at the sea but a bit higher up, surrounded by banana plantations. We found a lovely little two-story house which we share with another hippie family. We live on top, and they live downstairs. It had taken a while to find this place. When we first came, we had lived down here somewhere."

If it worked for them, why shouldn't it work for us? I asked him if he could keep his eyes open for something similar for us in Adeje and I'd pass by again over the next few days. I then went on to look for possible places to sing, and all in all I found about five more, which already made about ten in total. And I hadn't even asked in the restaurants yet. I tried to organize some appointments for playing the following night and each of them told me which time would be best for me to come and sing.

The next day I spent practicing and getting familiar with my new guitar. I was glad to see that Ruben had also put an extra set of guitar strings in the case. He had really thrown in a lot for that price. I took some time after lunch to meditate and shoot up some prayers, as I really felt I needed extra help and strength for this next step. I had never done any busking with a guitar.

The first place I went to sing was a pub, where people could eat fish and chips, and mainly drink. The owner had actually wanted me to start a bit later, but since I was already there he let me play. This was probably good, because people weren't that loud yet and they received it well. After about eight songs I passed the hat, and the owner then put something in too. I thanked him and asked if I could show up again a couple of nights later. This would give people a break, in case he had some of the same customers every night. "It went well; I could see people liked it. It's better than just listening to the hi-fi all night. It would be nice if you came again." His name was Jim, and he would later become a good friend of mine, even though he was not a hippie at all.

Out of curiosity rather than out of greed, I later counted what I had gotten together in the hat, and it was actually quite amazing. The night would continue like that and I enjoyed what I was doing and meeting many interesting people. I sang at about five different places that night and after getting back to 'Torres Del Sol', I went to sleep with that peaceful feeling that things seemed to be working out all right.

I kept singing for a couple more nights and was surprised how well the nights all turned out. My initial shyness had disappeared, and I started feeling a lot more secure in what I was doing. I also talked to the receptionist at 'Torres Del Sol', and they said that there were enough apartments free at this time of year; that I could just give a call once I knew when I was going to come again.

I went to find out when the ferry would leave to get back to La Gomera. Then I called Anne to let her know that I was going to come back the next day. I didn't want to just stay there and have her come over by herself, I wanted to help her carry her things, as well as to say goodbye to my friends there. So I had one more good night of singing, and realized that all the nights had gone extremely well, also financially. I also said goodbye to Eduardo and we agreed to stay in touch, and he wrote me down his address in Adeje.

When I got back home, Anne was waiting at the bus stop, as she knew when the bus would arrive. We fell into each other's arms, being so happy to be back together. We kissed and cuddled endlessly that night. In our discussions over the next couple of days, it became quite clear that we wanted to take that step, and that we had open doors. It was hard for us to leave this hippie paradise. We had spent one afternoon going around saying goodbye to all our friends. They were sad that we were leaving, but they understood and encouraged us for this move.

A couple days later, we were all packed up and ready to leave, waiting for the early bus to San Sebastian. Some of our friends had come over to say goodbye. Again there were lots of hugs as well as some tears. We had accumulated a bit more luggage, and we wanted to also take a couple of the paintings that Ruth had given us. We left two of them for Domingo and Carmela. Domingo insisted on driving us over the mountains to catch the ferry, and we even stopped for a while at 'La Laguna Grande', so that Anne could also get to know that magical place, and take a stroll through the rain forest, and touch and hug those beautiful and somewhat mysterious trees. Domingo had some tears in his eyes as well when we thanked him for all their wonderful help and for the nice times we'd had with them. We planned to call them sometimes to let them know how things developed. And so the three of us climbed the stairs of the ferry: Anne with her new life inside, and me.

As the ship was gliding over towards Tenerife, we saw the most beautiful sunrise. It was the first one we had seen since coming to the Islands. In Valle Gran Rey the sun would rise up from behind the mountains and that not so early. We had seen many sunsets, but now the sun was rising and signaling a new day and a new life.

We were holding each other's hands and Anne put her head on my shoulder as we sat there, and I could hear that voice again inside of me: 'You did the right thing'. I felt such peace and felt great appreciation for having received such clear guidance all along these past months while on this trip. Anne had her eyes closed and when she opened them, she looked at me with her warm smile and said: "Bernardo, I think we're doing the right thing."

About the Author

Sereno Sky will write a continuation of this story. You can stay informed at:

www.serenoskyproductions.com
http://serenosky.tumblr.com
Facebook: (https://www.facebook.com/pages/Sereno-Sky/700424796688861)
Twitter: (https://twitter.com/serenoskybook)